W9-ARB-507

Saint Peter's University Library
Withdrawn

PAINTING ∘ COLOR ∘ HISTORY

COLLECTION PLANNED AND DIRECTED BY

ALBERT SKIRA

ITALIAN PAINTING

THE RENAISSANCE

CRITICAL STUDIES BY LIONELLO VENTURI

HISTORICAL SURVEYS BY ROSABIANCA SKIRA-VENTURI

TRANSLATED BY STUART GILBERT

ALBERT SKIRA

GENEVA

© by Editions d'Art Albert Skira, 1951

*

Distributed in the United States by
THE WORLD PUBLISHING COMPANY
2231 West 110th Street — Cleveland 2, Ohio

OVERSZ
ND
622
.V4
[v.2]

THIS NEW VOLUME OF OUR COLLECTION 'Painting, Color, History' is devoted to the Renaissance, one of the most brilliant periods in the history of Italian painting. Throughout the XVIth century—quite rightly called the 'Golden Century'—a host of outstanding Italian artists raised, and offered solutions to, the great problems of art: feeling for nature, form, poetry, light, movement, color. An extraordinary series of masterpieces bears witness to the breadth and richness of their genius. Indeed, so abundant is the choice of remarkable works that, in setting out to illustrate the various aspects of Renaissance painting, we found our way strewn with delicate problems. That all were successfully solved is due, in large measure, to the warm spirit of co-operation shown by the Curators and Directors of the different Museums and Galleries, who so kindly put at our disposal the treasures in their keeping. We extend our most grateful thanks to them, and to Dr Eugenio Battisti who has given invaluable help in the ascertaining and verification of essential facts. Our thanks go also to the high ecclesiastical and civil authorities of the Vatican City and to the Minister of Fine Arts in Italy for their good will and assistance.

★

THE WORKS REPRODUCED IN THIS VOLUME WERE PHOTOGRAPHED AT THE VATICAN MUSEUM; SISTINE CHAPEL; LOUVRE, PARIS; MUSÉE CONDÉ, CHANTILLY; BRERA PINACOTECA AND AMBROSIANA, MILAN; DUCAL PALACE AND ACCADEMIA, VENICE; CHURCH OF SAN GIOVANNI, PARMA; GALLERIA D'ESTE, MODENA; PINACOTECA, BOLOGNA; PITTI PALACE AND UFFIZI, FLORENCE; GALLERIA BORGHESE, ROME; PRADO, MADRID; NATIONAL GALLERY OF ART, WASHINGTON; PINACOTECA, NAPLES; NATIONAL GALLERY, LONDON.

CONTENTS

LIST OF ILLUSTRATIONS

THE RENAISSANCE

BY

LIONELLO VENTURI

P.I. 2 — 1

LEONARDO DA VINCI (1452-1519). ISABELLA D'ESTE. (24¾×18″) DRAWING. LOUVRE, PARIS.

ACHANGE, and a highly interesting one, has been coming over the views of art critics and historians as to the true significance of the Renaissance. Yet even now, when the Italian painting of the sixteenth century is mentioned, we tend to conjure up, almost instinctively, a group of supreme artists, whose names resound through the ages: Leonardo and Michelangelo, Raphael and Correggio, Giorgione and Titian. And when we seek to know in what their greatness consists, tradition gives an unequivocal reply: these artists stand for the perfection of classical art, which moreover is *per se* the perfect art. For, we are told, all the ideals their predecessors, the artists of the Quattrocento, had set before them were realized so fully and magnificently by these men that their art could not conceivably be surpassed, and thus a decadence was bound to follow. And when, again, we are reminded that sixteenth-century Italy shaped the taste of the whole of Europe, it seems to follow that Italian art expresses the absolute perfection of classical art and also that sixteenth-century art is the only one completely representative of the Italian genius. And, lastly, since historians have placed in the sixteenth century the starting-off point of the modern era, we tend to see in Cinquecento art both the consecration of a final break with the Middle Ages and the first flowering of modern art. Thus during three centuries, up to the close of the nineteenth, it was taken for granted that the classical art of the modern age is the Italian art of the sixteenth century.

Nevertheless, of recent years, this conclusion has been questioned. What, especially, has been subjected to attack is the analogy so often drawn between the evolution of art and the successive phases of a human life—youth, maturity and age; thus nowadays far more importance is assigned to the individual genius of the artist. For it has been observed that Giotto and Masaccio are in no real sense inferior to Michelangelo, each being perfect in his own kind; nor does it follow that they prepared the way for Michelangelo. In short, Giotto and Masaccio have their own excellences, and not those of Michelangelo; and similarly Michelangelo stands on his own merits, without regard to those of Giotto and Masaccio. And this principle holds no less good when we wish to compare, for example, Piero della Francesca and Raphael, or Giovanni Bellini and Titian.

Thus each great sixteenth-century Italian painter can justly claim his own perfection; that is to say, a *perfection relative to the artist's individual genius* and to the conditions of the culture of his day; but not an *absolute perfection* as regards the artists who preceded or followed him. And their common greatness is not to be accounted for by any specious theory of the perfection of classical art, but by a study of the lives of the artists themselves and that of Italy at large during the sixteenth century.

To Giorgio Vasari (1511-1574) was due that theory of the "absolute perfection" of Cinquecento Italian art. His view was that the Quattrocento artists fell short of absolute perfection because they attached over-much importance to rules which cramped the artists' style; that is to say, the artist was discouraged from indulging in flights of fancy unauthorized by these 'rules' (though not actually infringing them). Whereas sixteenth-century artists displayed a marvelous inventiveness and a feeling for beauty down to the smallest details. While never losing sight of just proportions, as elements adding to the grace of figures, they did not stress them; when they drew the human body they did not lapse into that harshness of "flayed" forms which "both shocks the eye and ossifies the rendering," but, on the contrary, they treated it "with a gracious ease pleasing to the eye, and that softness of outline which we find in living flesh and bodies; and with exquisite tact they gave suppleness and grace to all their figures, especially women and children... making them plump and well-rounded, though without having that slightly ludicrous air they often have in nature, but transformed by the drawing and the artist's skill."

Leonardo, Vasari continues, initiated the Cinquecento manner, "that which we now call modern." "But he who amongst all living and dead artists bears the palm is the divine Michelangelo Buonarroti... He does not merely cast into the shade all those who, so to speak, have conquered Nature, but even those famous artists of Antiquity who, beyond all doubt, so laudably surpassed her."

Thus, to Vasari's thinking, sixteenth-century art transcended not only Nature but also Graeco-Roman art (which, likewise, in its way had surpassed Nature), because it had discerned a rule stemming from the creative imagination and excelling all rules based on mathematical proportions; because it lavishly invented, and skilfully invested all it portrayed with beauty, nuances, grace and charm. In 1898 was published Woelfflin's *Classical Art*, and his views still have currency. He endorsed Vasari's theory of the perfection of Italian sixteenth-century art, but justified it on new lines.

The sixteenth century, he says, applied the synthetic method as against the analytic method of the previous century; it stood for a new conception of human dignity, a new earnestness and elegance in the treatment of its subjects, going so far as to idealize the portrait. On the other hand it shows discretion in the rendering of expressions, nobility in its proportions and concentration of volumes; reverts to vertical and horizontal lines; simplifies details; gives a coherent lay-out to the composition; elaborates the representation with a variety of details and contrasting attitudes; makes the human body tell out in three-dimensional space; and so distributes light and shade on bodies as to bring out their modeling.

On the whole what Vasari and Woelfflin have to say is accurate enough so far as it goes, and if pure form, as apart from content, were all that mattered in art, their views as to the superiority of sixteenth-century painting would certainly be correct. Nor, indeed, can it be denied that it was owing to the importance they attached to form in itself that the Italians took the lead in European art during the sixteenth century.

But there is more to art than form alone, to the exclusion of content; in fact all form derives its value from a given content, that content being, in the last analysis, the spiritual outlook of the artist and the culture to which he belongs. And, when we look away from the splendors of classical form and toward the political, religious and moral conditions of the sixteenth century, the picture is very different.

From 1494, when Charles VIII invaded Italy, to 1530 and the fall of Florence, the Italian tragedy followed its disastrous course, ending with the loss of the country's independence, wealth and freedom. And whereas Quattrocento humanism had laid the intellectual foundations of the Reformation, Italy after a long and sometimes glorious resistance, succumbed to the Counter-Reformation. Also, whereas the prosperous conditions of the fifteenth century had prevented class differences from making themselves felt, the economic crisis of the next century brought these out in all their virulence. Thus at the very moment when her art reigned everywhere supreme, Italy herself was disintegrating.

That there was now a discrepancy between the outward form and the underlying reality of Italian life during this period is obvious. What was its nature and what were its consequences? Let us remember that three of the greatest artists of the century, Leonardo, Michelangelo and Giorgione never finished, never even wanted to finish, their works. The conditions under which they worked, the political and economic instability of the age were in part responsible for this, particularly in the case of Michelangelo. Yet the chief reason can be found in the outlook of the artists themselves: their feeling that painting and sculpture are 'mental' activities, their desire to differentiate themselves from the artisan, their aversion for the closed (hence restricted) form of picture or sculpture, estranging it from the universe. For they wanted to include the earth and sky in their portrayals; Leonardo, to adumbrate all the sciences of the future; Giorgione, to body forth his vitalistic dream of nature; Michelangelo, to break through the limitations of sculpture and pour the breath of life into solid matter. Each on his own lines, Leonardo, Giorgione and Michelangelo participated in the moral and intellectual ferment of their country and paved the way for new developments.

So we need not be surprised if this ever-present sense of grave responsibility hindered them from finishing their works in peace. On the other hand, it was just this feeling of responsibility that sponsored their unity of form and content, their commanding personalities and their greatness as artists. Whereas Raphael, Correggio and Titian had not the slightest trouble in finishing their works.

Raphael gave no heed to the tragic issues of his age, but lived for form alone; high-priest of Beauty, he kept his eyes fixed on the goddess he adored. Contemporaries held him for a super-man, and justifiably, for his art moved on a plane above man's everyday existence.

The beauty Correggio sought was more human, nearer the earth and rich in sensual appeal; sometimes gay and sprightly, sometimes languorous. A virtuoso, expert in a lore of strange enchantments, he lived for his art and had few dealings, save of a private order, with the outside world.

Titian, however, rubbed shoulders with the great: doges, princes, popes and emperors. He, too, was a magician but it was not so much beauty that he conjured up as an intensity of life, hitherto unknown. And life there is abundantly in his art, if treated from a worldly-wise angle, with an eye to stateliness, magnificence, and social eminence. Nevertheless we can feel the artist's detachment; he has no illusions about the life he portrays, but neither has he the least wish to interpret it in terms of any religious or moral code. And it is to this indifference towards spiritual values and to his faith in pictorial form that Titian owed that wonderful vitality we find in all his work and which constitutes his greatness.

The ways of art are manifold, and the masterpieces of the sixteenth century were the work sometimes of men who deliberately faced up to the moral and intellectual problems of the age; and sometimes of men who, deliberately ignoring these, shut themselves up in ivory towers and lived solely for their art.

Very seldom in the firmament of art has such a galaxy of varied genius appeared. Though their paths diverged or even took diametrically opposite directions, all these men had been schooled in the noble humanism of the previous century. Yet whether they flung themselves into the *mêlée* or kept aloof, all alike derived their greatness from the stand they took up as regards the life around them.

VASARI was happily inspired when he pointed to Leonardo as the precursor of the "modern movement" and all sixteenth-century art. For his coming marked the end not only of that naive idealism which we find in Alberti, and in the work of the Florentine fifteenth-century artists in general, but also of the faith in art as an instrument for uplifting the lives of men. To all such lofty pretensions—whether of a metaphysical, religious or even an artistic order—Leonardo gave short shrift; anything that tended to deflect the artist's immediate intuition of nature was to him anathema. Thus he applied himself to discovering the truths of nature, and this with a practical aim: of enlisting nature in the service of man. Though a man of science, a technician and a politician, he did not employ scientific methods; his intuitions in the field of science were of the same order as his artistic intuition. And it is this intermingling of art and science in his character which accounts for his fickleness, his tendency to swerve away from the work in hand. Thus we have any number of drawings by him, perfect of their kind, but relatively few finished paintings. As a scientist, he displayed a quite amazing prescience and boldness of conception; his ideas were centuries ahead of his time, he made blueprints for aeroplanes and submarines. Yet though he pointed the way to many great discoveries, he never brought any of them off. And in art, no less than in science, the aims Leonardo set himself proved to be impossible of achievement, given the conditions of the civilization of the age. For what he aimed at was nothing less than apprehending the secrets of the Cosmos by direct observation. The painter's task was to represent not man alone but the universe in all its manifestations; not merely the anatomy of man and the horse but the basic principles of movement and the mystery of the soul. And, in fact, Leonardo bequeathed to the world some amazingly pregnant works in which no aspect of movement and the soul was left unexplored; yet he failed to express the *whole* nature of movement and the *whole* human soul.

Thus it was he learned to distinguish between art and science. His approach to knowledge was of a scientific order and for this knowledge to become art two conditions had to be fulfilled. One of these is present in his drawings. In these we find brief, hastily if brilliantly recorded 'pointers,' but they are not worked out logically to a conclusion, not 'developed'; that is to say, they remain in the domain of intuitions, they are of the nature of those flashes of illumination which precede conscious ratiocination. Hence it is that Leonardo's sketches, with which *The Adoration of the Magi* has much affinity, have none of the completeness and precision of scientific drawings.

The second condition was that he needed to move on from the objective study of nature to the spiritual response, to the promptings of his temperament, to the cult of beauty, to a respect for the claims of the emotional side of his being. These were his moments of respite, intermissions in his advance towards an understanding of the world; and it was in such moments that he fell to painting.

Though his canvases were so few, his drawings known to so limited a circle, and his scientific writings remained unknown for three centuries, the influence of Leonardo's forms and conceptions made itself strongly felt at Florence, in Rome, Milan and Venice. He was universally regarded as the long-awaited pioneer who was to blaze new trails for Cinquecento art. This can be explained only by his way, peculiar to himself, of apprehending physical and psychical reality, and by his strictly objective approach to the visible world, unbiased by any preconceived ideals of beauty or goodness.

Viewed from this angle, Leonardo has much the same place in the world of art as Machiavelli in that of politics. And just as Machiavelli failed to realize his dream of re-organizing Italy, but none the less laid the foundations of a new theory of politics for all Europe—so Leonardo failed to realize his dream of penetrating all the secrets of the universe, yet laid the foundations of modern art and science. Neither of the two men did homage to the ethics of his day; that was the Faustian condition imposed on each, for the discovery of his world; and it explains the repugnance both men inspire both in persons of high moral principle—and in hypocrites.

It is significant, and perhaps saddening, to see how the youthful, carefree joy of the Renaissance has already vanished in even Leonardo's earliest works. Bright colors have given place to somber tones; clean-cut outlines to blurred lines that merge forms in an all-pervading dusk; the sunny morning light to the sadness of that dim hour when day is dying and night has not yet fallen. The crowd in *The Adoration of the Magi* is haunted by strange fears, in agonized suspense; its joy has changed to panic, as if some cataclysm were impending. And it was not without good reason that Pater read into La Gioconda's smile the sad, accumulated experience of untold ages of human sufferings and sins.

When after the fall of Ludovico il Moro, he lost all his belongings, all his pictures, and he had become a wanderer on the face of the earth, Leonardo wrote: "The Duke has lost his State, his possessions and his liberty, and no work for him has been completed." He voices no regret, no protest, and no pity, but coldly sums up the situation. When Italy was in the throes of dissolution, Leonardo gazed steadily towards the future; having set the course of all our modern art and science, he sought refuge in France, whither the French King had invited him, and where he died in honored peace.

STRENGTH, nobility and majesty—it is of these qualities we think immediately when we hear the name of Michelangelo, and since the form these take in his art is the heroic and sublime, we feel that, underlying it, is a spiritual drama, the unremitting struggle of a noble mind to find expression. This is something unique in sixteenth-century art, and it explains why the personality of Michelangelo stands above all others, even Leonardo's (though, intellectually, Leonardo was his superior); and above those of Raphael and Titian, though artistic creation came far more easily to them.

Michelangelo's career has curious contradictions. He aspired to be a sculptor and a sculptor only, yet some of his world-famous masterpieces are paintings or works of architecture. And his sculpture tells us more about the man himself than does his painting. While he doggedly pursued an ideal he had set up for himself, it did not wholly correspond to his personal, unavowed impulses; moreover many of his works were created for others and only some few for his own satisfaction. To the first class belongs the *David*, with which he made his reputation; of the second the most striking is the Rondanini *Pietà*, though the *St Matthew* and the *Prisoners* (at the Louvre) are likewise noble works. Never, perhaps, did he reach the same heights in his painting.

He studied in the 'Garden School' of Lorenzo the Magnificent and his approach to art was classical; thus he came at an early age to understand the statuary of classical Antiquity, the primacy of the structure of a carved body over its anatomy, and that quality of eternity immanent in works of antique art. Together with the classical outlook, he imbibed the Neo-Platonic doctrines that Cristoforo Landino, Ficino and the other humanists who frequented Lorenzo's court were then expounding. His poetic attachment to Vittoria Colonna and Tommaso Cavalieri was the outcome of this Neo-Platonic atmosphere of his early days.

Yet there is no denying that the quietism of the Neo-Platonists was unsuited to a man of Michelangelo's temperament, all for activity and movement. The Doni 'Tondo', though it represents the Holy Family, is essentially pagan in feeling; we see this in the fullness of the volumes and the nudes in the background. True, he draws his inspiration from Leonardo's *St Anne*, but his own driving force carries all before it. Similarly in the Sistine ceiling, volume and movement are everything; nevertheless the spirit of the Bible narrative has breathed life into these stupendous forms, has sublimated them. Virtuosity has sponsored a noble work of art. The movements rise spontaneously, the colors harmonize. In *The Creation of Adam* and *The Temptation* we feel a certain detachment in the artist's attitude; the beauty of the forms and the parts they play in the great drama of the world's beginning are perfectly balanced. Michelangelo's classical background accounts for the importance he gives to bodies, to relief, to the physical aspect of expression and to the release of the full potential energy of his creative impulse.

Yet it is clear that emotion was beginning to get the upper hand, leading him into realms unknown to the classical world. And the events of his life, the growing fervor of his religious sentiment, were weakening the thrall of classical culture.

His life was harassed by inner conflicts, divided purposes. He lived and prospered at the Papal Court, but, unlike Raphael, he had nothing of the courtier; far otherwise, he was always chafing against authority. In Pope Julius II he had a taskmaster no less self-willed than himself; however, they patched up their differences successfully. But it was another matter when Julius was succeeded by Leo X, a refined hedonist—and this new Pope feared the painter. Moreover though he owed an immense debt of gratitude to the Medici, Michelangelo never forgot that he was, first and foremost, a Florentine and a republican. And in Florence's fight for freedom he sided with the revolutionaries against the Medici and was even put in charge of the fortifications of the city. Momentarily, his nerve gave way and he fled to Venice; but soon a sense of honor brought him back to Florence, where he resumed his post, holding it until the city's fall. No sooner had he returned to civil life than he was summoned to work for Clement VII, a member of the Medici family, and being obliged to work for Clement intensified his sense of humiliation.

It is not surprising that his outlook on life became embittered; suffering himself, he thought that "all the world was weeping," and he put into the mouth of his statue *Night* the famous lament:

Caro m'è il sonno e più l'esser di sasso,
Mentre che 'l danno e la vergogna dura,
Non veder, non sentir m'è gran ventura;
Però non mi destar, deh! parla basso.

(Dear to me is sleep, but dearer the being of stone, While evil and shame persist; Not to feel, not to see, that is my good fortune. Nay, wake me not. Hush! Speak softly!)

It was this anguish ever rankling in his heart, that led him, in so many of his works, to emphasize movements, step-up expressions to a harrowing intensity, and to resort to an intricate, turbulent composition, far removed indeed from the classical spirit. Such was the mood in which he painted *The Last Judgement*, which has, not without justification, been regarded as a Baroque work.

Yet the mystical idealism which his contacts with Neo-Platonism had inculcated in him as a young man, memories of Savonarola's teachings which had greatly moved him, and the issues raised by the struggle against the Reformation on which the Pope, Paul III, had now embarked, led him to give anxious thought to his duties as a Christian. He was too conscientious to approve of the Counter-Reformation. Like Vittoria Colonna, Contarini and Giulia Gonzaga, Michelangelo took part in the 'evangelical' movement which aimed at a reform of morals and religious practice rather than a change of dogma—and was indeed one of the noblest products of Italian humanism.

It was in the throes of this religious crisis that he created his last *Pietàs*, in which we have an expression of his inmost feelings, illustrated by a gradual diminution of that bold relief in the rendering of plastic form which had won him fame in his young days. Architecture, however, did not lend itself to expression on these lines, and the cupola of St Peter's illustrates, rather, the art of the Counter-Reformation.

In Michelangelo are summed up all the formative elements of the life of his age: the youthful exuberance and optimism of its classical ideal, accesses of vigorous but unavailing political revolt, evangelicism as against the Counter-Reformation and authoritarianism—but, none the less, a willingness to bow to the inevitable. Such self-contradictions, repentances, and evasions are lapses to which even a deeply sincere religious temperament is liable.

We look in vain for a man of Michelangelo's caliber among his contemporaries; to find one we must go back several generations, to a time when strong characters and strong passions were not exceptional—to the days of Dante. Michelangelo and Dante have often been likened to one another and, due allowance made for very different historical conditions, not unjustifiably. In their lofty moral conceptions and their intense desire to embody these in art both stand out as more-than-human figures.

BEFORE taking refuge in France, Leonardo had met with no success in the Papal Court of Leo X; how indeed could his desperate quest of the impossible have been appreciated, when beauty, charm, perfection were within arm's reach, fully achieved in the work of Raphael?

All great art assumes two aspects—that of the possible and that of the impossible. Raphael's contemporaries saw in him only the first aspect, and were loud in praises of his genius, the beauty of the Roman ladies who were his models, the vivacity of his portraits, the sumptuousness of his color. Most of those who, in later days, put Raphael on a pinnacle far above all other artists, saw him from the same angle as his contemporaries; for them he represented not only the finest flower of the Renaissance, but that high refinement which characterized the Court of Leo X, when the Goddess of Beauty, who had manifested herself in Greece in the fifth century before Christ, had once again deigned to visit the earth.

Most art-critics, up to our days, while echoing this general enthusiasm, have found some trouble in giving reasons for it. Vasari recognizes that Raphael ranks below Leonardo "in those portentous depths whence rise the concepts and the grandeur of art," and is inferior to Michelangelo "in coping with difficulties of all kinds" and in perfect rendering of the nude. For Vasari Raphael's perfection lies in his skill in rendering "narratives with happy ease, and their vagaries with intelligence," and embellishing them "with perspectives, edifices, varied and fantastic landscapes"; in his delightful way of dressing his figures and "making the faces of young and old people, and of women and children, lively and attractive by imparting to them flexibility or boldness, as the case may be." He admires Raphael's lifelike portraits and their brave array, his effects of moonlight and sunlight. Though Raphael lacks Leonardo's intellectual eminence and Michelangelo's formal perfection, Vasari has a fondness for him because he shares in our life here on earth, shows us so many aspects of it, and effortlessly lends charm to all he touches. We gather that, to Vasari's thinking, modern art was inaugurated by Leonardo and Michelangelo, and Raphael adorned it; if Florence was the heart of Italy, Urbino crowned her with exquisite luster.

The opinion of Woelfflin, an eminent authority on representational art and one of the moderns whose loyalty to Raphael remains intact, should be quoted here. "Raphael has not Leonardo's nervous sensibility, still less the power of Michelangelo. Perhaps we might say that the distinctive quality of all he set his hand to is his feeling for measure, for the 'golden mean.' That personal charm of manner which captivated all who came in contact with him, is still manifest today in all his works." And, speaking of *The Dispute over the Holy Sacrament*, he says: "Here it is in the effect of the picture as a whole that the beauty lies. The arrangement of space, the interlocking of the figures in the lower part of the fresco, the nobly soaring movement of the curve formed by the company of the Saints, the contrasts between the attitudes of movement and those of calm—all combine in a work of art that has been often pointed to as the supreme example of the majestic religious style. Yet what gives this work its ultimate appeal is its happy blend of youthful diffidence and hardy vigor; these interact without ever clashing." Thus we may say that a sense of measure, a skilful lay-out of space, diversity of attitudes, youthful timidity combined with strength, and other allied qualities characterize Raphael's art. But these alone would not account for the exalted place assigned him by a long tradition, and indeed we feel instinctively that there is more in him than this; that, besides possessing these eminently rational virtues of just balance and the like, he, too, aimed at an 'impossible' peculiar to himself.

Another difficulty we have in understanding Raphael is due to our modern insistence on 'originality'. Leonardo made his apparent from the start, when he collaborated with his master Verrocchio in *The Baptism*; in the case of Michelangelo it is hard to trace the influences of any given master in his early works. Raphael died young and throughout his brief career he owed much to others: Perugino, Leonardo, Michelangelo, Sebastiano del Piombo (to name only the most eminent figures), and this was why his contemporaries thought—and Michelangelo is said to have endorsed this view—that his art was more the product of study than of natural talent. Here there was obviously a misconception; artistic creation does not necessarily mean inventing, and Raphael metabolized into a personal 'constant' all the styles that he assimilated; thus there is nothing of the 'variation on set themes' in his art. Yet this lack of coherence in the succession of styles adopted seems puzzling in the case of an artist regarded for many centuries as the greatest of all painters.

If we are to solve this problem and detect in Raphael's art that element of the 'impossible' which raises it so to speak above itself, we need to bear in mind the state of Italy between the years 1500 and 1520, a period of national disintegration. It seemed as if Italy had gambled away her religious, moral and civic heritage. The Italians centered their devotion on art, on poetry, on beauty, to the exclusion of all else. And while Italy herself was invaded and conquered, she, in turn, conquered Europe with her art and poetry; that is to say, by dint of her aesthetic tradition and reproductions made available by engraving, and by grace of a culture based on rules and customs which, though they gradually ossified, were still full of life at the start.

The prime condition of every truly artistic culture consists in an attention to form apart from content, in the vitality imposed into form-in-itself, in a cult of art for art's sake. And if ever a man practiced art for art's sake (or, as Gautier put it, "for beauty's sake") it was Raphael.

This points the way to the academy, and indeed Raphael was the founder of that ideal academy which in time became the academy of all Europe, lasted several centuries, and exists today in our training schools. An academy is repetitive in the sense that it copies time-honored models, rather than aspiring to creation. But this creation of the academy—in other words a formal paradigm that was to hold its own for centuries—was in itself a work of art, and the credit for this is Raphael's.

Raphael's form has not the intellectual content we find in Leonardo's, nor Michelangelo's moral fervor; yet it has a vitality peculiar to itself and, giving scope to free inventive fantasy, is less academic than creative.

Raphael was a hot-house flower, and that hot-house was the Court of Urbino, forcing-bed of the 'perfect courtier.' And the Court of Leo X implemented the ideal formulated at Urbino. Raphael was a handsome young man, diffident but amiable, a witty talker, a good table companion, and also something of a *grand seigneur*. He rode around the town, followed by his retinue of pupils. Thus he embodied a social ideal, that of a community interested above all things in art. Moreover the carefree hedonism of the life in the Italian courts, the absence of high moral standards, had the aesthetic merit of discouraging propensities to idealism, and encouraging the artist to give formal beauty a warm, palpitating life.

For the academy form meant plastic form, and this, owing to its lack of color, pointed painting's way towards abstraction. Raphael, however, was a born colorist. He stepped-up Perugino's color, but subsequently, at Florence, out of deference to Leonardo and Michelangelo, curbed this tendency; his works of this period are his coldest, most sophisticated, and least alive.

But, in Rome, the work of Sebastiano del Piombo and the Venetians revived his enthusiasm for color; and now his color became more sumptuous, more varied, at once more fanciful and more ingenious, as against the color-schemes, lavish as they were, that he had employed at Perugia. And Raphael transformed the color he took over, steeped form in it and infused it into form, though without following the Venetian practice of making the color *per se* create the form. *The Mass of Bolsena* is Raphael's masterwork, as a colorist.

The vitality of the academic ideal of art for beauty's sake, the transmutation of form into color—all these are aspects of a style persisting, despite frequent variations and caprices, throughout Raphael's work. To define this constant of his art, one cannot do better than quote the words of Raphael's friend, Baldassare Castiglione, when he discusses the quality of 'grace.' "Seeking to ascertain whence came this grace, which touches with a star-born light all those who have it, I lit on a general principle, which seems to me more applicable than any other to all that men say and do. It is that we must give as wide a berth as possible to that dangerous reef on which so many founder: *affectation*; and, if I may use a word that perhaps is new, we must practice in regard to all things a certain detachment *(sprezzatura)*, which conceals all artifice or art, and suggests that what we do or say comes to us quite naturally, without our giving thought to it."

'Detachment' as regards life and the world, effortlessly almost unthinkingly practiced—that is the secret of 'grace,' and that is Raphael's secret. And we do well to pause before deciding that this seems too trivial a factor to account for the art of one of the world's greatest painters and the climax of Renaissance culture. For surely in this consists that subtle dividing line which must be crossed for talent to blossom into genius, prose into poetry, and for life to be sublimated into art.

ANTONIO ALLEGRI, known as Correggio, from the name of his birthplace, is still famed for his charm, his delicacy; and a sensuality so subtle that all we notice is its elegance and grace. We do not expect from him the intellectuality of a Leonardo or the moral sense of Michelangelo. He comes nearer to Raphael, and perhaps the best way to an understanding of this delightful painter is a brief survey of his differences from, and similarities with, Raphael.

Since the Middle Ages a principality under the rule of the Princes of Correggio had existed in the small town of that name. Thus Antonio Allegri, too, was of provincial extraction. But, from the cultural angle, Urbino, Raphael's birthplace, was much more advanced than Correggio. Allegri had the benefit of the same Quattrocento formation as that of the Ferrarese painters and Mantegna. Like Raphael, he learnt much from Leonardo's art and followed Michelangelo's lead by broadening his manner. Thus in his case, too, extraneous influences did much to shape his style; nevertheless, he gave a personal imprint to a form that had a happy knack of assimilating any content that presented itself. But here his affinities with Raphael end; today no critic would deny that Raphael's form is of an altogether higher intellectual order.

One reason for this difference may be that Correggio spent nearly all his life in the provinces, far from the great artists from whom he drew inspiration, and whose works he probably saw only in reproduction, or rather summarily. For though he visited Florence and Rome, he did not stay in either city as long as Raphael. But besides this material factor, there was another, implicit in his temperament: a sensuality which gave his art its driving force and constantly impelled him to be as much an artisan as an artist, and it is this that gives his work a more direct and obvious appeal, though less elevated, than that of Raphael.

For two centuries Correggio's popularity at least equaled that of Raphael. Though connoisseurs might give the palm to Raphael, more seventeenth- and eighteenth-century artists imitated Correggio; indeed during the eighteenth century there was nothing short of a cult of Correggio's 'grace,' so much so that one of the founders of Neo-Classicism, Mengs, while paying homage to Raphael's divine talent, frankly admitted that he preferred Correggio.

Moreover, as he survived Raphael by fourteen years, Correggio had ample time to shake off the yoke of traditional Renaissance art, and to try his hand at the Baroque method of rendering movement; his two Parma cupolas are unquestionably the finest examples of Baroque decoration, and the same is true of the altarpieces, notably the *Madonna of St George*. Though these innovations are the most important from the viewpoint of the historian of taste, it is not in these works that we see Correggio's creative genius at its splendid best. For that we must look back to earlier works such as the *Campori Madonna* at Modena (in which color, form and tender emotion are perfectly fused together) and the *St John in Patmos*, in which the forms created in a rigorously closed space, the intensity of color and vigor of attitude show at once an inventiveness and depth of feeling that have never been surpassed. Similarly, the suavity and sweetness which so rightly won the admiration of the artist's contemporaries and successors, are not so much to be found where he made a point of stressing them; for delightful as they are, they are effects deliberately aimed at, as in the Magdalen in the *Madonna of St Jerome* altarpiece at Parma. We find them at their best in his pagan subjects: *Danae, Io, Ganymede* and *Leda*. Here, so delicately conceived are the proportions that he might be painting the bodies of children rather than those of men and women; the vibration of the light is modulated so as to bring out the soft texture of the flesh; the color, reduced to a delicate tenuity, suggests more than it reveals—in a word, Correggio attains in these works the legendary beauty of Renaissance art at its most exquisite.

Correggio was born and lived near Ariosto, and the sensual grace he conjures up resembles that of Ariosto, though the poet had a sense of classical harmony combined with a soaring fantasy that brings him nearer Raphael than Correggio. But so absolute, so sufficient to itself is the perfection (within the limits we have indicated) of Correggio's art, that he is rightly ranked amongst the greatest masters of the Renaissance.

SAINT PETER'S COLLEGE LIBRARY
JERSEY CITY, NEW JERSEY 07306

IN THE LONG, eventful annals of the Venetian Republic, the years 1500 and 1510 stand out as the most disastrous. Venice was being attacked by the whole world, by the Pope no less than by the Emperor, and it was only by desperate efforts she succeeded in surviving.

Even in those years of storm and stress a young painter, Giorgio da Castelfranco, found time to gaze lovingly at the woods, the fields and streams; they inspired him with an almost sensual enthusiasm, so much so that he came to regard the human form as a part of nature, bound up in nature's life. Contemplating the beauties of the world, he was ravished with delight, but saddeded when he remembered that all this loveliness must pass away; then, in an uprush of emotion, he would take up his lute and sing the praises of the god he adored, the natural world around him.

It is interesting to note that the buyers of Giorgione's pictures were the young scions of the Venetian aristocracy, who wanted them for their private collections. Hitherto orders for pictures had come from the authorities, churches, confraternities and the 'Schools.' The younger generation of 1500 found these visions of an all-encompassing love, the curious enchantments that Giorgione's art imparted even to sticks and stones, greatly to their taste. For a new world, due to the social conditions of the day, was now being opened up to art; a world of exquisite sensuality imbued with romantic yearnings, of landscapes composed in terms of color and its infinite gradations. And thus, when Giorgione died in 1510, a new form of painting had been born in Venice.

Reality as Venice understood it in those days, and as it figured in Raphael's art, had no place in Giorgione's vision of the world. His craving to transcend the human image, to treat it as engulfed in the totality of things, justifies us in regarding him as the artist who achieved, spontaneously, the ideal of Leonardo, painter of the Universe. To do this Giorgione had recourse to a new kind of form—chromatic or pictorial form. Giorgione's teacher, Giovanni Bellini—in, for example, his portrait, *Doge Loredano*—sharply defined outlines so as to give his picture the semblance of a colored statue. Leonardo had done away with these strongly demarcated contours, softening them off in such a way that the transition from one form to another seemed unbroken. Nevertheless his mistrust of colors prevented him from imbuing his forms with them. Giorgione, however, benefiting by the richer chromatic practice of his day, realized how much could be done with color if the gradations of light and shade were incorporated in it—not for producing effects of modeling by way of chiaroscuro, but for imparting to every tint a specific function in terms of light and shade. He was in fact the discoverer of what we now term 'values'—a discovery destined to play so large a part in subsequent art. Thus it was discovered that color could create its own form.

And, after Giorgione, Venetian painting used this color-light for creating the image enveloped in the atmosphere and merged into its environment rather than isolated and circumscribed like a work of plastic art. Moreover this color-light was not limited to the representation of fluid or ethereal substances; it also enabled the artist to express those supreme, mystical moments when, in a sudden access of love, he could feel at one with all creation and breathe a divine life into it. Thus Giorgione's innate pantheism, his love for all natural things, directly led up to the discovery of 'values' in painting.

In his creation of this new, purely pictorial form, Giorgione was venturing into the world of the future; hence the indecisions, the retractions and the tendency to leave a work unfinished that characterize his art.

None the less this new, intuitive vision of nature fascinated the younger generation; they even bought Giorgione's unfinished pictures and had them completed by his disciples, Titian and Sebastiano del Piombo—which goes to show they appreciated the qualities of the artist, not merely those of the accomplished craftsman.

It is hard to conceive of anything less intellectual than a scene by Giorgione; in it nature reveals herself in all her naked loveliness, and the human figure is merged into the artist's sensuous vision. But Giorgione's sensuality has not the illustrative quality we find in Correggio, who chiefly refined on, and perfected, an accepted mode of painting.

The painters of the day were wont to seek poetic inspiration in contemporary or ancient literature (Botticelli's *Primavera* is a case in point) or else in mediaeval poems, lending the glamor of romance to their religious themes (e.g. Giovanni Bellini's *Souls in Purgatory*). Giorgione, however, painted 'tales' which floated up from his own inner consciousness, and, in adapting them to the exigencies of his art, left them, so to speak, in the air. Thus in *The Tempest*, he transformed a naked woman walking beside the stream into a vague soldier, so as to balance the composition and to add a note of mystery to the leafy nook in which the gipsy is suckling her child. That a woman bathing should be deliberately changed into a soldier proves that there was no fixed subject in the artist's mind; this is borne out by other works and by Vasari's admission that he could not make sense of the figures at the Fondaco dei Tedeschi.

Giorgione, in fact, reduced the subject to the *motif*; he wished the phantoms he conjured up, visions of romantic youth, to look natural, but he did not trouble to weave them into a myth or story; to render his dream-figures with precision—that was his one aim. And this, it should be noted, was one of the greatest discoveries ever made in art, a happily inspired step towards the conquest of freedom in painting, as well as an example for all future artists of the combination of splendor of execution with daring fantasy.

Many were his imitators, but all lagged far behind their great precursor. His dream was too personal, too peculiar to himself, for others to be able to share in it.

NO MORE than a year after Giorgione's death, in his paintings at the Scuola del Santo at Padua, Titian gave evidence of a style distinctively his own. Ended, it seemed, was the age of dreams; an age of action, and the glorification of action, was beginning. It found expression in a new ability to render forms in motion—moving freely in space—and this gave a new immediacy to the portrayal; it was as though the whole body were actuated by an impulse all the more potent as its size was greater. And this was done through light-and-shade effects, in which shadows, richer and more elaborate than Giorgione's, gave movements a value exceeding that of the figures themselves. Here we have the beginnings of that 'cosmic movement' which was to characterize the art of Titian's last phase.

For works of this order, the artist needs congenial subjects, and ones which lent themselves to treatment on dramatic lines were always those that suited Titian best. Now and again he dallied with young, beautiful figures—but these remained outside the main stream of his art. In the picture known as *Sacred and Profane Love* (in the Borghese Gallery), however, the theme is of the vague, puzzling kind that Giorgione liked; the figures, one nude, one fully dressed, seem to melt into the spacious, smiling landscape; everything here speaks for a rapturous delight in the whole of nature. The execution is more assured than Giorgione's, the pictorial elements are larger, the chromatic effect no less striking. Yet we somehow feel that behind this obvious splendor there now is nothing; that keen desire for intimate communion with the life of nature which we found in Giorgione has passed away; we cannot help being conscious of a certain superficiality. Indeed we have an impression that Titian, in his early days, aspired to paint the visions of a dream, but without himself surrendering to dreams; yet it was, in fact, this detachment that enabled him to make the most of his stupendous talent.

In his next phase religious themes and dramatic methods of treatment play a large part. His *Assumption of the Virgin* (c. 1518) is the most grandiose expression of his mature style. Actually, however, Titian had no genuine religious feeling, only a profound respect for the State religion, whose grandeur, dignity and beauty deeply impressed him. The figures move as freely on earth as in the sky, and we are always conscious of their superhuman powers. These effects are the result of an ever bolder handling of light and shade. Yet it is not when Titian indulges most freely in the rhetoric of movement and the grandiose that he is at his best. Rather, it is when he concentrates upon his inner vision; then the movement is held in leash and plays a constructive part—as exemplified in the Ancona altarpiece (1520) and the *Pesaro Madonna* in the Church of the Frari, Venice (1519-1526). Meanwhile with his portraits Titian was winning the high esteem of the nobility of Italy, of the Emperor, the King of France, the Pope. These portraits were, at the time, quite a new departure. Notably, they did not give (like those of Raphael, for instance) a merely abstract rendering of Space and Time. In Titian's art the essence of the portrait consists in the gesture, in the movement; the form is not self-contained but open, its life is shed forth upon the world. Thus what we find in his portraits is more than a mere likeness; it is the instant presence of life that he brings home to the spectator. And whether plain or handsome, all the figures in his portraits have a certain moral tone.

Quite suddenly, it seems, Titian made the discovery that to express their greatness, blacks and greys would serve him better than yellow, red or green. Thus it was that between 1520 and 1550 one of the world's greatest colorists attained the peak-point of his art by the use of black and grey.

A reciprocal admiration existed between Titian and the *élite* of the age; he was given the patent of nobility and made Count Palatine. No Cinquecento painter was more illustrious, and he accepted honors as his due, with an odd mixture of familiarity and deference: an attitude borne out in his art, portraits and religious themes alike.

After the men's portraits came those of beautiful women in the guise of Venus, Danae, and their like; and, in the contemplation of these comely forms, the painter's respect gave place to an almost religious veneration, finding its expression in warmer tones.

Several times in the course of his career Titian came under the spell of Michelangelo and tried to imitate him—to the detriment of the cohesion of his color-form technique. After 1550 he never left Venice. In his old age he was always needing more and yet more money, but he now ceased counting on his painting to fill his purse; he painted exactly as it pleased him. Suppressing more and more the outlines of his forms by the primacy accorded color, he imparted to their volumes a vibrant, atmospheric quality, blurring the gradual transitions from one mass to another. At the same time the color, already fined down to its purest statement, emerges or retreats in compliance with light effects of his own devising which, no longer controlled by the physical laws of representation, conform to an inner law of personal expression. Thus Titian was the discoverer of our modern 'luminism,' the 'luminism' of Rembrandt. And in this consists, undoubtedly, the new element introduced into painting by this ' magician of color,' to the stupefaction of Vasari who could not make up his mind whether to praise or to condemn a way of painting he had never dreamt of.

But this 'magic of color' was the outcome of a special state of mind; the painter who had been in such close contact with the rulers of the day at the time when they were crushing out all freedom of thought and embarking on a struggle which was to steep Italy in blood during the next century, knew only too well that the civilization of the Renaissance, the golden age of his young days, was drawing to its close. And, given his keen sensitivity to artistic form, Titian realized, too, that Renaissance art must now be superseded, and thus he pointed the way to Baroque luminism. This enabled him to express, in his safe retreat in Venice, the anguish of all Italians as they gazed anxiously towards the dawn, dark with forebodings, of a new century.

LEONARDO and Michelangelo, Raphael and Correggio, Giorgione and Titian were born before 1500 and had imbibed the notions of the Quattrocento. Verrocchio and Ghirlandaio, Perugino, Mantegna and Giovanni Bellini had taught them that what matters in art is not the copying of appearances, but that the artist should endeavour to get down to the very essence of reality by the exercise of his creative imagination. This imaginative element was, in fact, the hallmark of the artist's style, but all these men were aware that, in the last analysis, it was reality they represented.

It was their unquestioning faith in art and in reality, shared by all artists in the early years of the Cinquecento, that enabled them, even in youth, to attain a characteristic equilibrium and impart to their imaginings a solid, firmly delineated form—the 'classical form' as it was then described, and was always so described when looked to as a model in the succeeding centuries.

Leonardo died in 1519, Raphael in 1520 and Giorgione in 1510—too soon for them to feel any doubt about the indivisible unity of art and nature; but Correggio, who died in 1534, and *a fortiori* Michelangelo and Titian who died in 1564 and 1576 respectively, lived long enough to be affected by the growing spirit of unrest and the tendency to challenge all established views, political, religious, moral and scientific. This explains why their art differs so much from that prevailing in their youth, and we find Michelangelo and Titian setting up their personalities against the world rather than aligning them with it. Artists who were born after 1500 were acclimatized to doubt and a sense of detachment as regards the outside world. They had no trouble in mastering the stylistic subtleties of the masters, but regarded these rather as technical devices than as means of interpreting what they saw around them. The link between style and nature was broken; what counted most for these artists was the elegance of elongated forms, carefully thought out poses. Known as 'Mannerist,' this new school treated forms with a slightly morbid sensuality combined with an extreme intellectualism, and we see its negative side in its rejection of ideal symbols in favor of new forms of expression born of the artist's free-roving imagination. Its positive aspect was its quest of novel sensations in line with the new moral and intellectual exigencies of the age. Pontormo (though born in 1494), Bronzino and Parmigianino were, amongst others, pioneers of Mannerism. Pontormo was at once its protagonist and its victim, for he carried it to an extreme limit; nevertheless, with the deep concern for religion and morality we find in it, his art is much more than merely Mannerist. Bronzino toyed with the ideal of an abstract perfection, sometimes making it a directive of his art, sometimes treating it as no more than a matter of good form. Parmigianino made his own the experience of Raphael and Correggio, and handled what he took from them with an adroitness and elegance that earned the well-deserved approval of the dilettanti.

Towards the middle of the sixteenth century Mannerism spread everywhere, proliferating from its chief centers, Florence, Rome and Parma. At Venice, too, it had many adepts, and indeed was a determining factor in the art of the greatest masters in the second half of the century: Tintoretto and Paolo Veronese. In Venice, however, some great artists followed Giorgione and Titian in sponsoring a new theory. After imparting to Raphael himself the new way of seeing the world that was Giorgione's, Sebastiano del Piombo assimilated Michelangelo's drawing so marvelously that some of his contemporaries saw in him Michelangelo's *alter ego*. His actual aim, however, was to ally Michelangelo's drawing with Venetian color; an attractive program, which found many advocates amongst the writers and art-critics of later generations. Lorenzo Lotto stands out as a man of a thousand-and-one experiments in art, not only on its aesthetic side, but also in its religious and moral applications. And he ably solved these problems, embodying his discoveries in his art not only with outstanding inventiveness and ease, but also with a goodness of heart that does him credit. Indeed it was this combination of sterling moral qualities and his instinctive, wholly human response to all that he saw in nature that prevented Lotto from becoming a Mannerist, and enabled him to carry to their highest pitch those 'luminist' light-and-shade effects which Titian attained only later.

Meanwhile Savoldo was specializing in certain 'luminist' procedures inaugurated by Giorgione, and he adjusted them to the expression of his personal vision of everyday reality. Between 1530 and 1550 Florentine and Roman Mannerists often worked at Venice, where Parmigianino's elegance was in high favor, and where that vigorous, if bombastic, artist, Pordenone, was stressing the plastic qualities of his work so as to vie with Titian's.

And, meantime, Tintoretto's precocious genius was coming into its own.

TINTORETTO drew inspiration from several masters, applied himself to studying the paintings and sculpture of Michelangelo and was particularly interested in Titian's handling of color. By 1545, when he had made good a personal style, his knowledge of the technique of representation was prodigious, yet apart from his purely visual gifts his general culture seems to have been limited, there was always a touch of the plebeian in his approach to art.

At the very time when the distinction between the artist and the artisan was gaining strength in Italy and leading artists were coming to feel a class-pride in their calling—Titian was made a Count Palatine—this artisan of far-ranging genius made his appearance on the Venetian scene.

Yet wereas the merit of the artisan is evaluated by the care he devotes to the 'finish' of his work, Tintoretto was censured for his 'carelessness' from the start. Still, while advising him to improve his drawing, both Aretino and Vasari agreed in praising his vivacity and intelligence: "the most astounding brain that painting has ever known." Actually, it was just this fact of being an artisan as well as an artist that enabled Tintoretto to open out new paths to art; after Michelangelo and Titian, painting called for this new, craftsmanly approach, enabling the creative impulse to show itself in each individual brushstroke. For when painters, not content with the 'touch' *per se*, tried to build it up in terms of traditional composition, so that, spreading out, it melted into form and color, it necessarily lost its force as a vital element of art.

Tintoretto took as his raw materials Michelangelo's form, Titian's color and the formal procedures of Mannerism, but he did not share in the life whence he drew these elements; thus he reduced artistic *motifs* to methods of pure craftsmanship. Starting solely from these premises, "the most astounding brain," despite the studies and research-work that lay behind, proceeded to create in happy freedom. How heavily their culture weighed on the Mannerists! Well, on Tintoretto's shoulders nothing weighed. His art, we might almost say, was 'art with the brakes off.' That is why he had nothing to gain by improving on his sketches; they were life-size, and, in fact, finished pictures. Some have thought to see in this merely the whim of a virtuoso; on the contrary, it was due to a compulsion of his creative imagination. Not all Tintoretto's works are masterpieces; but surely an artist who, in the space of fifty years, creates a whole new world for art, has the right to occasional lapses. We must not forget that, had he not created by hasty touches, dashed off, it seems, on the spur of the moment, that world would never have come into being. It is the world of Luminism under its boldest aspect; that art-world which found such favor in the next century, especially with Rembrandt, and later on with the Romantics and Expressionists. Tintoretto looms large amongst the harbingers of boldness and freedom in painting.

Yet a harbinger, great as he may be, may fall short of being a great artist. What then is the spirit that breathes life into these light-bestowing touches?

There was nothing in Tintoretto's make-up to lead him, like Titian, to frequent the great men of his age. He had the outlook of a 'man of the people' and took no interest in the moral and religious conflicts of the Reformation and Counter-Reformation. Though, after the first upheaval had died down, peace did not return to Venice, the latent fissures were camouflaged under the trappings of tradition. The Church was the State Church, and so deeply rooted was the veneration of the populace for the Church that it had become essential to their lives. Naturally Tintoretto shared in these feelings, and he had no doubt as to the validity of the great religious themes, their transcendent, supernal values. Yet— was it because he had seen so many portrayals of them?—he treated them with familiarity, and took liberties with them to an extent that the Primitives had rarely, if ever, allowed themselves. But always, just at the point where vulgarity is on the brink of creeping in, Tintoretto saves the situation with a touch of that happy gift of fantasy which never failed him. And we are reminded of a remark of Ruskin's that there is not a stone, a leaf, a shadow, there is nothing whatever, however trivial, that does not assume the value of "an oracle." An oracle, no doubt, but not a vehicle of magic.

What makes Tintoretto's strength is his faith in the reality he is creating; even those elements of it which might seem absurd are invested with a more-than-human import. That is why this artisan of genius developed into a wonder-working artist. Under his rapid touches, those sudden, unexpected gleams of light of which he had the secret tell out all the more strongly for the surrounding gloom, as at night a lightning-flash seems to us brighter even than to noonday sun. And like the lightning, the divine light comes suddenly, charged with revelations. Thus Tintoretto's light is full of revelations to those who do not gaze at it through the deflecting prism of Neo-Classicism.

WE NEED TO visit a sacred edifice, at San Rocco, to understand Tintoretto; to understand Paolo Veronese, an official edifice, the Doge's Palace. Many painters worked there, but the aesthetic tempo is set by Veronese. Born at Venice, Tintoretto lived beside the church of San Rocco and the divine world within it. Whereas Paolo was born at Verona, a dependency of Venice, and, though he was still young when he came to the capital, his character had already been shaped by his provincial upbringing. What impressed him when he set eyes on Venice was the splendor of her pageants, the dignity of her life, the magnificence of Venetian attire, the grandeur of her palaces and terraces, the lordly gestures of her citizens—all the pomp and luxury that were the glory of the island Republic in the sixteenth century. We must also remember that while Tintoretto's outlook was that of a man of the people, Veronese, though the son of a stone-cutter, was one of nature's aristocrats, and it is an aristocratic realm we enter through his canvases.

When in 1573 he was summoned before the Inquisition, for having included in his *Feast in the House of Levi* ('The Last Supper') figures of Germans and buffoons, he explained that painters, like poets and madmen, are entitled to a certain *licenzia* and he had to "adorn" his pictures as he thought best. Actually (except towards the end of his life) the true content of his pictures did not consist in the religious themes they professed to illustrate; hence the vast success enjoyed by his huge scenes of feasts, with their display of typically Venetian luxury—and also the lack of any heartfelt emotion in his portrayals of Christ. His last great work was consecrated to *The Glory of Venice* (in the Doge's Palace); it would be true to say that his whole output, whatever the ostensible subject might be, was a homage to the glory of Venice.

This 'joyous worldliness' we find in his art was bound up with his conception of color-form. At Mantua where he had studied the new Mannerist procedures, these were less influenced by the art of Giorgione and Titian than by the Mannerism prevailing in Venice round about 1550. The Mannerists used forthright colors; 'values' played no part in the harmony of the picture. We have already pointed out that Titian, at an early stage, took to reducing his color-schemes so as to enhance the effect of the values. Veronese, however, retained the full range of colors indulged in by the Mannerists; he had recourse to values only when he wished to stress a color and flood it with light without lowering its chromatic intensity. Shadows he disliked, and he transformed them into a light penumbra, so as to give light the widest scope. It is his extraordinary feeling for color—in its scintillating raptures, its hesitancies, its clouded silences—that constitutes his greatness and gives him a unique place in the history of art.

The world of his imagination is inseparable from his conception of color. If, as Tintoretto saw it, God's light is a lightning-flash in the darkness, Veronese knew that the light of Venice is sunshine flooding everywhere, under porticos no less than on the terraces. And in his enthusiasm for the life of his day, he imparts to his colors a buoyant rhythm that broadens out and recurs again and again on surfaces often of vast extent, and without a qualm he abandons themes and procedures favored by his contemporaries. Thus he abandons movement; by a dexterous handling of perspective he makes his figures live in space, but he gives them movement only to make good an attitude, so as to balance them within the limits of the picture, and he moves up all foreshortenings into the foreground. Also, though he knows well the technique of rendering depth, he is interested chiefly in the surface, the two dimensions of his canvas. Thus most of his pictures consist of a series of images in the foreground, set off by a background of architecture and a sky blazing with light.

All this is handled with an effortlessness, a bland detachment and a serenity unique in the age he lived in. It is this serenity which has led to talk of Veronese's 'classicism,' and to his being assimilated to the more poetic artists of the Renaissance. A mistaken view; Raphael, who was earnest in his serenity, would never have dreamt of likening the artist to a "madman"; Veronese did this so as not to have to face reality; *his* serenity is the calm after the storm. The 'divine' qualities in man no longer stirred the imagination and Veronese gratified his taste for graceful gestures, fine garments and imposing colonnades.

Whereas Tintoretto had those who understood and imitated him in the Seicento, it was not until the next century that Veronese was at the height of his renown. Yet, if painting was given a new lease of vigorous life in Seicento Venice, this was, almost certainly, the work of Veronese, who was the promoter and chief exponent of the new painting.

As the years passed Veronese, too, not only came to a deeper understanding of himself but also to feel the tragedy of the times; some of his crucifixions and *Pietàs* are deeply moving, unspectacular, imbued with tender sympathy. And in his rendering of a beautiful woman, half swooning in a mystical ecstasy, we feel, beneath the artistry, very real emotion. These works, however, are exceptions, indeed something of a surprise; but they are of interest as showing the underlying humanity of his outlook on the world.

With his display of pomp and luxury Veronese cuts the figure of a *grand seigneur* drawing the curtain on the Renaissance. All around him the old conventions were breaking down; Jacopo Bassano placed his Madonnas and Saints amongst the sheep and cows of the Bassano marketplace; Moroni's masterpiece was his picture of *The Tailor*—this sort of subject appealed to him far more than the provincial nobility and the lives of the Saints.

Such was the close of the Renaissance. The divinity of man, hymned by Masaccio with a faith in man perhaps unique in history, had passed away. Divinity had withdrawn itself into a world supernal; the Church alone had a right to intercourse with it. On earth, it was Bassano's sheep that counted....

HISTORICAL SURVEYS

BY ROSABIANCA SKIRA-VENTURI

A NEW OUTLOOK ON THE UNIVERSE

LEONARDO DA VINCI

DE PREDIS · SOLARIO · BOLTRAFFIO

PIERO DI COSIMO · ANDREA DEL SARTO

MICHELANGELO AND THE SUBLIME

MANNERISM · PONTORMO AND BRONZINO

TOWARDS AN IDEAL BEAUTY

RAPHAEL

CORREGGIO AND PARMIGIANINO

*

THE VENETIAN PAINTERS

1

GIORGIONE THE POET

TITIAN AND REALITY

2

SEBASTIANO DEL PIOMBO · LOTTO · SAVOLDO

BASSANO · MORONI

3

TINTORETTO, PAINTER OF LIGHT AND MOVEMENT

VERONESE AND THE TRIUMPH OF COLOR

P.I. 2 — 2

—   —

LEONARDO DA VINCI (1452-1519). SELF-PORTRAIT. (13×8¼″) RED CHALK. BIBLIOTECA REALE, TURIN.

A NEW OUTLOOK ON THE UNIVERSE

LEONARDO DA VINCI

★

DE PREDIS · SOLARIO

BOLTRAFFIO · PIERO DI COSIMO

ANDREA DEL SARTO

LEONARDO DA VINCI (1452-1519). MADONNA AND CHILD. (10½×9″) DRAWING. LOUVRE, PARIS.

LEONARDO DA VINCI

From the start of the fifteenth century to its close, from Masaccio to Botticelli, Florence had been the home—whether in the literal or in a spiritual sense—of a quite amazing number of great artists. Boundless energy, a keen desire for knowledge, a firm intent no less to revive the glories of Antiquity than to annex the future—such were the motives that sped the men of the Quattrocento on their quest. The painters had taken up enthusiastically the study of perspective and discovered the secret of rendering light in terms of color. During the second half of the century that remarkable man Lorenzo de' Medici— financier, merchant, clear-visioned statesman—had ruled the city's destinies, and to him Florence owed a period of great prosperity, relative stability and high hopes for her future. Himself a man of letters, he made his court a unique cultural center; a generous patron, he fostered high achievements in the field of art. The last years of his rule, however, brought premonitions of the changes and the ordeal Italy was to undergo in the next century. It has been said that Lorenzo assured his glory by a well-timed eclipse, for the year of his death (1492) marked the end of the city's power. Savonarola's sermons had sown doubt and despair in the hearts of Florentines. With Botticelli, painting evoked the languor and despondency of the age; in his last works we have a poignant cry of grief for the darkness that had fallen on a bright, regretted world. It was Leonardo's art that opened windows on the coming century.

Born in 1452 at Vinci, a village near Florence, Leonardo was the illegitimate son of one Ser Pietro and spent his childhood in the home of his grandfather. As a youth, he was taken up by the Medici court and worked in the famous gardens at the Piazza San Marco, surrounded by the magnificent collection of works of art the prince had brought together. Young Leonardo could hardly have hoped for more stimulating surroundings, more favorable to ventures in all fields of artistic and scientific research. There the greatest artists of the day forgathered, Verrocchio, Pollaiuolo, Botticelli, Baldovinetti, Filippino Lippi, Ghirlandaio, all employed and protected by Lorenzo the Magnificent.

Having enrolled in the painters' guild in 1472, Leonardo entered Verrocchio's workshop. At once a painter, sculptor, goldsmith and perhaps an architect as well, Verrocchio had a wonderful way with young artists and launched many on successful careers. Leonardo and his master were leagues apart in temperament and this, perhaps, has given rise to the story, endorsed by Vasari, of a keen rivalry between the two. A serious-minded, perhaps over-cautious artist, Verrocchio sought with a certain harshness of line to achieve a mastery of his subject-matter and fidelity to the thing seen. But already in his share of the *Baptism of Christ*, Leonardo revealed that predilection for landscape backgrounds and graceful attitudes which made itself felt in all his later art.

When he speaks of Leonardo in his *Lives of the Painters*, Vasari almost uses the hushed tones of a man before an idol or a god. Beauty of person, brilliance of mind, and skill in all fields are attributed to him. One fault is found: "Had it not been for his changeful and capricious temperament, he would have gone far in the *Belle Arti*. He began many things, then left them unfinished." This reproof was made Leonardo time and again throughout his life. When he moved from Florence at the age of thirty, he left behind two unfinished paintings: the *Adoration of the Magi* and *St Jerome*. It may be suspected that he welcomed his departure as a pretext for leaving the pictures as we have them today. Happily unfinished, says Berenson, speaking of the *Adoration of the Magi*. In both of these works we find a spirited handling of line, a living quality in the light playing on the figures, and an atmosphere charged with mystery that none before Leonardo had been capable of suggesting. The world depicted in the art of his day was self-contained, fixed, circumscribed. Leonardo set out to break the shell and to evoke movement, and his chiaroscuro renders forms with an infinity of nuances. The Madonna, in his *Adoration of the Magi*, a focal point and source of light, seems to be borne forward by the broken patterns of the crowd, moving in dim half shadow,

LEONARDO DA VINCI (1452-1519). STUDY FOR THE ADORATION OF THE MAGI. (10¾×8″) LOUVRE, PARIS.

while the landscape emerges from an infinite recession, mysterious depths of distance. For Leonardo 'finishing' a work meant petrifying, immobilizing, forms of being whose very life stemmed from their mobility. Already in these two works, belonging to his first Florentine period, he may be said to have achieved his life's ideal.

According to an anonymous Florentine of the sixteenth century, Lorenzo de' Medici sent Leonardo to the court of the Sforzas at Milan in 1482. A letter from the artist to Ludovico il Moro is extant, in which he submits a variety of proposals for that prince's consideration. He offers to construct a great variety of war material, light but sturdy bridges, catapults, mines, armed vehicles and the like; in peacetime he will turn to architecture, the building of aqueducts, the erection of statues and similar works. Eager to attract the greatest artists to his service and thus enhance his fame, Ludovico leapt at the offer. He was much impressed

LEONARDO DA VINCI (1452-1519). THE ADORATION OF THE MAGI. (95½×96½″) UFFIZI, FLORENCE.

LEONARDO DA VINCI (1452-1519). THE ADORATION OF THE MAGI (DETAIL). UFFIZI, FLORENCE.

by Leonardo: a genius, a painter "whose like we have never seen," a man bubbling over with ideas, initiative, inventiveness. The newcomer was soon busy organizing festivals (for Ludovico loved display), blueprinting new *palazzi*, beginning work on an "immense bronze horse" for an equestrian statue, and doing portraits of the Duke's favorites. During his stay at Milan, Leonardo was constantly engaged in work of the most varied descriptions.

The first of his finished works which has come down to us is the *Virgin of the Rocks*. This was commissioned in 1483 and Leonardo and the two De Predis brothers worked together on it. The contract called for quick delivery and set forth in detail the subject to be represented. None of the conditions was fulfilled and work dragged on for many years, punctuated by the painters' request for money. Two versions of the subject are extant: one at the Louvre, the other, probably the later version, at the National Gallery in London. It is generally agreed that, in the latter, most of the work fell to the De Predis, while in the great picture at the Louvre we find all of Leonardo's most characteristic traits. His chiaroscuro bathes the figures in a soft light that dies away into a fathomless dusk, while sudden gleams bring out faces whose indefinable, far-away espression seems to tell of a life in some strange other world, emerging from the cavernous blue of the landscape. Here Leonardo is seeking to render the incessant vibration of the air; and building up forms and bodies in an atmosphere of quivering tenuity. He does not try to explain or find a solution, but to permeate his vision with the primal mystery of nature. Thus Leonardo gave art that foothold in a realm of the infinite which sponsored the great developments of the sixteenth century. Leonardo's was a scientific mind, engrossed in mathematical research, never happier than when computing and constructing. Yet he played his full part in art and the magnitude of his creative effort is incalculable. Whence the undying glory of his name— and also the blame he incurred for leaving so much unfinished, for trying his hand at too many things and carrying none through to the end.

Some observations made by Leonardo in his famous *Treatise on Painting* may well refer to *The Virgin of the Rocks*. "Light, darkness, colors, relief, figures, position, remoteness or nearness, movement or calm repose—these are the ten adornments of painting." When we remember that, from the days of Masaccio on, the painter made concrete reality his starting-point for taking flight into the world of abstraction, we can understand what a vast field of inspiration lay open to Leonardo in the manifold reality of nature. And in ardently seeking to penetrate, so to speak, its inmost soul, his adventurous spirit, ever athirst for new discovery, led him to go beyond all limits hitherto assigned the artist, and confront problems undreamed of by the painters of the Quattrocento.

Elsewhere he writes: "Observe how in the evening, when the weather is rainy, the faces of the men and women you meet on the roads acquire a singular grace and gentleness." Thus in the atmosphere of Leonardo's pictures we find personages who seem to be inviting us to read intuitively the mystery behind their looks and smiles...

A universal genius: thus he strikes us still today. Dazzled though they were by his abilities, his contemporaries could not appreciate the full depth of his art or its philosophical insight. What impressed them was the charm, the elegance of his work, as is evidenced by the remark Isabella d'Este made when asking him to paint a picture of the young Christ: "I would have you give Him the sweetness and suavity of expression in rendering which you excel."

Generally speaking, what the artist was most reproached for was his dislike for working methodically, the immense time he spent on research-work, and his constant discontentment with what he did. Thus the qualities which we in our days regard as the well-spring of his genius were precisely what his contemporaries singled out for attack. "He set to studying philosophy, and was so crammed with ideas and quaint conceits that, despite all his skill, he could never paint aright," wrote Castiglione, stupefied by Leonardo's audacities.

One of his most famous works is the *Last Supper*, in the refectory at Santa Maria delle Grazie at Milan, on which he worked in 1497. "The memory of this worthy man," wrote Stendhal, "has a poignant interest when we remember that, of those three great works,

LEONARDO DA VINCI (1452-1519). THE VIRGIN OF THE ROCKS.
(78×48″) LOUVRE, PARIS.

the *Last Supper*, the gigantic horse and the cartoon for the *Battle of Anghiari*, nothing is left to bear witness of him to posterity.'' Those of his contemporaries who saw these works in their pristine state were thunderstruck, loud in admiration. Owing, however, to the medium employed—tempera on a wall surface—the *Last Supper* went rapidly to pieces. Its state today is such that no real appraisal of the work is possible and, as André Malraux has remarked, we are obliged to include it in the "privileged class of glorious ruins."

Of particular interest, in this connection, is an eyewitness account of the artist at work on the *Last Supper*, which has come down to us from Bandello, a well-known author of *novelle*. "Leonardo often came to work at an early hour of the morning, and promptly clambered up on to the scaffolding, for the *Last Supper* is situated at a considerable height above the floor; his practice was to work brush in hand until late in the evening, taking no thought for food or drink, but painting without cease. Then two, three or four days would go by without his touching his brush, though he spent one or two hours daily gazing at what he had done; he was turning it over in his mind, ruminating and debating with himself... Yet I have also seen him (when the mood took him) come in at mid-day, take up the brush, give a few dabs to one or two figures, turn and go off again."

This rather casual, lordly manner of going about his work would seem to answer to one facet of his character. For we are bound to note that the fresco in Santa Maria delle Grazie is not quite free of a certain theatrical touch in the movement of the groups. Keeping to his conception of the functions of light and shade. Leonardo tended to impart a new psychological validity to individual attitudes, till then virtually ignored in art, but exploited thereafter by all painters, from that day to this.

A friend of the artist, the mathematician Luca Pacioli, wrote of the *Last Supper*: "How amazing is the accuracy with which the apostles have been glimpsed at that very moment when the divine voice utters the terrible truth: One of you will betray me!"

Although busy painting and devoting much time to scientific experiments concerning weight and motion, Leonardo also contributed to the Duke's war efforts. But the downfall of the Sforzas was at hand, with the French troops entering Milan on March 16, 1500.

Prudently Leonardo had made plans the year before for his departure. In one of his notebooks we read: "The Duke has lost his State, his possessions and his liberty, and no work for him has been completed." He turned his steps towards Venice, stopping on the way at Mantua, where Isabella d'Este was trying to raise her court to the brilliance of those at Florence and Milan. Devoted to art—her 'studio' contained works by the foremost painters of the time—she enthusiastically welcomed the Florentine artist, and their friendship continued until 1506. Her letters are full of references to Leonardo's doings after his leaving Mantua and after his brief stay at Venice.

It was in the summer of 1500 that he arrived in Florence. When in 1501 Isabella d'Este asked for news of him, her correspondent wrote: "Leonardo's life is so erratic and wayward that he appears literally to 'take no thought for the morrow.' All he has done since coming to Florence is a sketch on pasteboard [this is the Saint Anne in the *St Anne, the Virgin and Child*]. And even this sketch has not been finished. Just now he is wrapped up in geometry and shows no wish to paint."

From 1502 onward Leonardo put his services at the disposal of the 'dragon' Cesare Borgia. In his capacity of 'Architect and Engineer-in-Chief' he traveled often in the Romagna; even after his return to Florence, he was much taken up with military projects. These multifarious activities did not prevent him from undertaking, in competition with Michelangelo, the vast *Battle of Anghiari* fresco, which was to decorate a wall fifty yards long and ten yards high in the Council Chamber of the Palazzo della Signoria. The 'cartoon' (probably never completed) was begun in 1503, and a contract for the painting of the picture was concluded with the artist the following year. In 1506 Leonardo left Florence after having painted only the central group, the *Battle of the Standard*.

To recognize the limits of his own powers was not Leonardo's way. What he always aspired to was the infinite, the grandiose, the impossible. The more he succeeded in bodying forth his inspirations the more dissatisfied he was with the results, and the more he tended to leave his projects merely sketched out or only partially finished. Not that he ever lost faith in his ideal, but, perceiving the inevitable gulf between the ideal and its realization, he was ever chafing against the limitations

P.I. 2 — 8

LEONARDO DA VINCI (1452-1519).
LA GIOCONDA. (30¼ × 21″)
LOUVRE, PARIS.

—

LEONARDO DA VINCI (1452-1519). MADONNA, THE VIRGIN OF THE ROCKS (DETAIL). LOUVRE, PARIS.

LEONARDO DA VINCI (1452-1519). ANGEL, THE VIRGIN OF THE ROCKS (DETAIL). LOUVRE, PARIS.

inherent in all art. In the *Battle of Anghiari* fresco, trying out elaborate technical procedures, he only succeeded in making the colors run and ruined a whole section of the work. His creative genius never felt at home within the bounds of human possibilities. And the fact that we find among his drawings some of the most perfect achievements of his art, is explicable by the greater freedom drawing allowed of. It was, however, judging from the accounts of his contemporaries, 'that welter of men and horses' in the Palazzo which filled them with admiring wonder more than any other of Leonardo's works.

From preparatory sketches, copies of the fresco and documents relating to it, we are able to gather some idea of its magnitude as a work of art. The surging mass of horses and riders was contained in a well-knit, pyramidal lay-out holding together the medley of conflicting movements, tensions of onrush and recoil.

The *Saint Anne* at the Louvre is another instance of his predilection for monumental structure, achieved here by tectonic passages of light and shade and by what has been described as "the interpenetration and interlocking of actual atmospheric masses." Also belonging to this second Florentine period is the famous *La Gioconda*. According to Vasari the model for the portrait was Monna Lisa, wife of Francesco del Giocondo. Few pictures, perhaps none, have given rise to so much speculation as this, poets, writers and critics of all ages plying their imaginations on this woman and her mysterious smile. Sphinx-like, she gazes forth from the infinite depths of a landscape melting into a blue-green haze and bathed in an otherworldly evening glow.

In 1506 Leonardo left Florence and returned to Milan. There he was welcomed by the French governor, Charles d'Ambroise, who held his abilities in high esteem and intervened several times on his behalf when the Florentine authorities demanded his extradition to that city, claiming that the artist "had accepted a considerable sum of money and completed only a fraction of a large work" (this in reference to the *Battle of Anghiari* fresco). Later on, it was at the personal request of Louis XII that Leonardo remained in Milan. And when that monarch visited the city, he appointed him 'painter and engineer in ordinary' at a fixed salary. We know, however, little of his activities from this time until his departure for Rome (September 24, 1513). He seems to have devoted himself largely to studies in anatomy and to projects concerned with watercourses in the country districts of Lombardy.

Leonardo was sixty-one when he came to Rome and entered the service of Giuliano de' Medici, brother of the Pope Leo X. And although Giuliano thought highly of him, the Pope did not. Nor were other circumstances in his favor, for the artists most in the public eye were Raphael and Michelangelo, and the latter had no great liking for Leonardo. He now applied himself to architecture and engineering projects, and busied himself with writings which he later drew on for his *Treatise on Painting*. During this period his output in the field of art was scanty—and this intensified the Pope's hostility.

At the death of Giuliano in 1516, he left Rome. His notebook tells us that he was in France in May 1517, and had settled at Cloux, near Amboise in Touraine, a residence of the king, Francis I.

There he spent the last two years of his life, held in high honor by all around him and enjoying the friendship and admiration of the king. Though he took part in organizing the brilliant festivals held at the court, he tended more and more to withdraw from the world, and became increasingly absorbed in meditation and study, with the result that his activity as an artist was still further curtailed. In the month of October, 1517, the Cardinal of Aragon paid him a visit, accompanied by his secretary, Antonio De Betisa, who wrote as follows: "We called on the Florentine, Messer Leonardo da Vinci, who is more than seventy years of age and the greatest painter of our time. To His Excellency he showed three pictures, one representing a Florentine lady, painted after nature at the request of the late Giuliano de' Medici, another of St John the Baptist when young, the third of the Madonna, with her Son sitting on St Anne's lap—all very beautiful. Yet, as things now are, we can expect of him no more masterpieces, for he is suffering a kind of palsy of the right hand..." It is recorded that during Leonardo's last illness King Francis often visited him. On the first of June 1519 the King, who was with him, trying to ease his pain, took the dying painter's head in his arms. Then, as Vasari describes it in his picturesque way, "Leonardo's divine spirit, recognizing that he could not enjoy a greater honor, expired in the King's arms."

Gazing at that drawing of an old man in the Turin Museum, accepted as Leonardo's self-portrait, we can see why he often struck his contemporaries as being far older than he actually was. Like some legendary seer, he seems to have glimpsed the great *arcanum*, the hidden meaning of the universe.

LEONARDO DA VINCI (1452-1519). DRAPERY STUDY. (10×9¾") DRAWING. LOUVRE, PARIS.

LEONARDO DA VINCI (1452-1519). ST ANNE, THE VIRGIN AND CHILD. (67 × 51″) LOUVRE, PARIS.

44

★

Leonardo's revolutionary discoveries had an unparalleled influence on the art of his age. Though he himself wrote that "no one should imitate another artist's manner, because then he would be a nephew, not a child, of nature in his art," his habit of deducing laws of art from his personal intuitions lent his ideas a pedagogic value.

Even if we set aside the fact that his pupils often closely collaborated with him, the directive spirit of his art left so strong an imprint on them that his name comes to our lips again and again when we see certain of their works—even though these have all the individual characteristics of the pupil in question. Such paintings as *The Musician* in the Ambrosiana at Milan or the famous *Belle Ferronnière* cannot be positively ascribed to De Predis and Boltraffio respectively, so close is their kinship with the art of the master himself. Obviously, whatever view we may take, their value as works of art is not affected. However this proves, amongst other things, how close was the link between Leonardo and the new school of painting. In fact this observation holds entirely good for Milan only. It is not known if Leonardo actually had a studio there, but it was at Milan that he found the artistic climate most favorable to the development of his genius, and it was there that he rose to highest fame. Thus the impact of his art on that of following generations was more decisive in Milan than in any other Italian art center. True, his art did much to stimulate the growth of a new kind of painting in Florence, too; but the Florentine painters were at once more individualistic and stemmed from an old, firmly rooted cultural tradition; thus they were not drawn to the art of Leonardo so readily and whole-heartedly as were their Lombard contemporaries.

Leonardo's visit to Milan marks a break in the indigenous tradition of Lombard painting, which (as for example in the work of such men as Foppa and Borgognone) had some highly interesting qualities. Indeed it would seem that the influence exercised by Leonardo at Milan was too overpowering for painters who associated with him fully to extricate their own personalities. One thing is sure: that his presence opened new horizons, new portals of discovery. Woelfflin remarks that "it was above all owing to its sweetness that the art of Leonardo made such an impression in Lombardy." The nuances of chiaroscuro and the curious, otherworldly atmosphere that bathes Leonardo's figures take the form, with his successors, of an accentuation of their more superficial characteristics. We find the same smile, the same grace and a like elegance of treatment, but the expressions of the faces now conjure up a more simply human world. And in some cases this led to regrettable results: indeed the reef on which much of the painting that came after Leonardo foundered was its inability to create a new world, and its tendency to lapse into the sickly-sweet, the mawkish. But these unfortunate developments took place chiefly during Leonardo's second stay at Milan. During his first (which lasted about fifteen years), his influence made itself felt over a more restricted field, and perhaps struck root more deeply.

Amongst the Lombard artists who drew inspiration from him, De Predis came closest to the master; Andrea Solario, who was also influenced by Venetian art, learnt much from the personal teaching of Leonardo, while Boltraffio in his work gave Leonardo's style a more academic trend.

Ambrogio De Predis, Leonardo's first collaborator, was commissioned in 1483 to paint, together with his master, *The Virgin of the Rocks*, and the association between master and pupil was obviously a close one, since the former was living at this time with the De Predis brothers, and Ambrogio's name occurs in all the records relating to this picture. Little is known of his life. He was born in 1455 or thereabouts, and his name crops up in records up to 1508. An illuminator and medal-maker, he was attached to the court of Ludovico il Moro previously to the coming of Leonardo to Milan. In 1493 he was at Innsbruck, at the court of the Emperor Maximilian, of whose wife (Ludovico's niece, Bianca Maria Sforza) he had

?AMBROGIO DE PREDIS (C. 1455-?). PORTRAIT OF A MUSICIAN. (17 × 12″) AMBROSIANA, MILAN.

made a number of portraits. Besides his commissions for portraits of court notables, he designed new coins for the imperial mint. In 1494 he was back at Milan, where some years later he was employed on making designs for tapestry.

The only work known for certain to be his is a portrait of the Emperor Maximilian, dated 1502. This suggests that De Predis had then returned to the Emperor's court. In 1506, back at Milan, he applied for an estimate for the second version of *The Virgin of the Rocks* and, two years later, received the balance of the sum due on this work.

So scanty is our information regarding this painter's career, and so few are the references to his work in records of the time, that it is hard to picture the man as he really was. The efforts of art historians have been directed to isolating a group of works of the same style, which presumably he painted by himself. His share in the London version of *The Virgin of the Rocks* is not a true expression of his personality. In fact De Predis seems to have been essentially a portrait-painter. His figures, usually in profile and treated medal-wise, tell out, stately and serene, against a shadowed background. In fact they carry on an old tradition of the art of Lombardy, linking up with the productions of Late Gothic. Their metallic glints, the use of a harsher light in the deep tones, give the faces he paints an expression very different from that enigmatic grace we find in Leonardo's faces. In the portrait-study of *The Musician* the characteristics of both pupil and master are apparent in the rendering of a figure strongly circumscribed by the clean-cut drawing, yet enveloped in a subtle play of light and shadow ranging from the face to the warm tones of the costume.

Andrea Solario did not actually study under Leonardo, though the thematic elements of his painting are closely allied to those of Leonardo. He was a many-sided artist and struck out in new directions. Born in or about 1470, he hailed from a small town near Milan, and several members of his family were artists. About the year 1495 he visited Venice, where his brother Cristoforo, sculptor and architect, was living; his altarpiece for the church of S. Pietro Martire at Murano was made in 1495. To the influence of Venetian art (apparent in this picture and persisting in his later work as well) is due a tendency towards the fusion of forms and colors which obviously derives from Giovanni Bellini.

In the *Lady playing Lute* the balance of the composition and the means of expression chosen by the artist impart a real dignity to the picture. Solario set much store on color; he wished it to be sumptuous, but refined and subtly graduated, and the way he distributes his gracefully yet clearly delineated forms in space shows much skill. It may help to an understanding of Solario's art if we regard it as tending towards a synthesis between the art of Leonardo and various Northern and Venetian influences.

On his return to Milan he came in contact with Leonardo, with the result that he began to give more thought to the structural lay-out of his composition. He also made a trip to France about this time and did some work in the chapel of the Château de Gaillon; the chapel no longer exists, but an old guide-book gives some account of the work he did in it. It has been said that from his visit to France he brought back a taste for sober elegance, and also something of the new tendencies of Flemish art. He died in 1524.

Though sometimes we cannot help feeling that his art suffers from this plethora of influences, there is no question that Solario, notably in his portraits, combined a feeling for tradition with a broadness and vigor of composition justifying his claim to rank as far more than a merely derivative artist.

Unlike Solario, Boltraffio tended to follow Leonardo's lead throughout his career. He was born in 1466 or 1467 and died in 1516. We know little of his life. Such records as exist show that his high merits as an artist were recognized at the Court of Milan. Apparently he took to art fairly late in life. In 1491 he was working in Leonardo's studio, a circumstance on which he evidently prided himself; for, when signing an altarpiece (in 1500), he added: "Pupil of Leonardo."

His master's influence is evident in a large group of his works, especially in the half-length portraits and Madonnas, in which the modeling of volumes is emphasized by elaborate transitions from light to shadow, against a dark background. However, Boltraffio often

BOLTRAFFIO-LEONARDO. LA BELLE FERRONNIÈRE. (24½ × 17¼″) LOUVRE, PARIS.

betrayed a tendency towards mannerism in his handling of forms, and in the use of colors tending to be over-suave. Yet sometimes we see him following his master's lead, to the happiest effect: as in the Ambrosiana Museum drawing. Here the quiet dignity and restrained emotion of the woman's face are deeply moving, while a subdued lighting enhances the rapt serenity of her gaze.

ANDREA SOLARIO (C. 1470-1524). LADY PLAYING LUTE. (29½×22″) PALAZZO VENEZIA, ROME.

PIERO DI COSIMO (1462-1521). THE DEATH OF PROCRIS. (25 × 71½″) NATIONAL GALLERY, LONDON.
REPRODUCED BY COURTESY OF THE TRUSTEES

PIERO DI COSIMO

In his *Surrealist Manifesto* André Breton said that the artist's model should always be that which is perceived with the mind's eye alone. This notion of a type of painting governed by the artist's uncontrolled imagination and exploring realms of the 'superreal,' was foreshadowed many centuries previously in the art of Piero di Cosimo the Florentine, born in 1462. So unusual often are his subjects, so queer the creations of his wayward fantasy, his visions of a world in which men and animals blend into each other, that he appears to have a gift of creating solely with the imagination, without a trace of 'imitation.' Yet though there is no question of the singularity of his art, we can trace in it a connection with that insatiable thirst for knowledge so characteristic of the Renaissance. Thus the pioneers of the new culture did not limit their field of investigation to the Christian era; nor did they merely recall to life the forms of classical Antiquity. They also aimed at 'a fusion on the emotional plane between the pagan Past and the Christian Present' (Panofsky).

In early youth, collaborating with his master Cosimo Rosselli, he painted the frescos in the Sistine Chapel. According to the contracts the work was to be completed in 1482, and we may assume that master and pupil were back in Florence by that date.

Piero's work, it seems, was essentially of a decorative order, and he may have been asked by Lorenzo de' Medici to assist in organizing the pageants which took place so frequently in the years 1487 and 1488. He also painted *cassoni* (marriage coffers), and the records tell us of mural decorations made for private houses. For the 1511 Carnival of Florence he decorated the 'Car of Death,' of which we have a detailed description from the pen of Vasari, and later took part in decorating the triumphal arches erected in honor of the visit of Pope Leo X. In 1521 some friends found his dead body lying on a staircase.

In his account of Piero di Cosimo, Vasari dwells on the artist's curious temperament, his misanthropy and inability to come to terms with the world. Thus he led a life "more bestial than human," shut himself up for days, refusing to see anybody, and let his garden run quite wild—forms of eccentricity which have counterparts in his paintings, in which, too, we see nature at her wildest encroaching everywhere, queer animals disporting themselves in a riot of huge-leaved vegetation and man himself, his body cruelly distorted, ceases to be a superior being gifted with intelligence and becomes a denizen of the animal world.

Striking is the diversity of inspiration in Piero's art. Many of his pictures deal with religious subjects, but mythological scenes are frequent, too. Four panels illustrate the human story up to the end of the Stone Age; elsewhere we have hunting scenes and bacchanalia (as described by Ovid), showing the revelers discovering honey and wine.

PIERO DI COSIMO (1462-1521). LANDSCAPE, THE DEATH OF PROCRIS (DETAIL). NATIONAL GALLERY, LONDON.
REPRODUCED BY COURTESY OF THE TRUSTEES

PIERO DI COSIMO (1462-1521). LANDSCAPE, THE IMMACULATE CONCEPTION (DETAIL).
UFFIZI, FLORENCE.

The Death of Procris is one of his most characteristic works, not only by reason of the purity of the style, but for its poetic rendering of the contrast between the ugliness and injustice of death, the havoc it makes of all human beauty, and the serene, aloof indifference of nature. Of Piero di Cosimo's portraits, that of *Simonetta* (in the Chantilly Museum) is one of the most famous. The snake entwining the gold necklace the young girl is wearing and the thunder-cloud in the background symbolize her tragic destiny.

Vasari described Piero di Cosimo's art as "fantastic and full of ideas," and indeed with its bold imaginativeness it strikes a curiously modern note.

PIERO DI COSIMO (1462-1521). LA BELLA SIMONETTA. (22¼ × 16½″) MUSÉE CONDÉ, CHANTILLY.

ANDREA DEL SARTO

It is chiefly the romantic side of Andrea del Sarto's life, with its legendary glamor, that has made his name familiar to the general public, while his reputation as a painter has undergone some curious vicissitudes. He was regarded by his contemporaries as one of the very greatest artists of the day: an opinion that most modern critics are reluctant to endorse, though not denying that he was a painter of considerable originality.

He was born in 1486 at Florence, his father being a tailor—hence his name—and after being employed for some years, as a boy, in a goldsmith's workshop, he went to study in Piero di Cosimo's *bottega*. Vasari says that "Andrea could not stomach the eccentricities of Piero, who was then quite old," and indeed their paintings show that temperamentally the two artists were poles apart. His earliest works are dated 1510; the famous *Madonna of the Harpies* was completed in 1517. Next year he visited the court of the Kind of France, where he had an enthusiastic welcome. But his stay there was short; he could not bear being away from his wife Lucrezia, whom he had married in the previous year. According to Vasari, she had a very bad influence on her husband—but we may suspect that he is voicing a personal dislike for Lucrezia. This is the origin of the romantic legend attaching to his life. On his return to Florence he was snowed under with commissions: for frescos at the Villa Poggio a Caiano, for altarpieces, for numerous pictures mostly of religious subjects, and a few portraits. He died in 1530.

Contemporaries saw in him a peer of Raphael and Michelangelo, and the vast renown he once enjoyed obviously owes much to the praises heaped on him by such authorities as Vasari and Borghini. Yet even in these eulogies we find hints of the less favorable view of his art that was, later, to be taken. Thus Vasari, while praising Andrea's color, chiaroscuro and fidelity to life, observes: "Had he but made proof of a stronger, bolder character, on a par with his talent and inventiveness, he would certainly have been without a rival as a painter."

And writing in 1591, Francesco Bocchi said: "Though Andrea is not greater than Raphael in his use of soft yet lively color, nor profounder than Buonarroti in his drawing, he is certainly incomparable in his handling of strong relief, in vivacity, in his rendering of natural objects. And since all these are found in nature, Andrea is not only equal in this respect to Raphael and Buonarroti but indeed superior to both."

During his 'prentice years (if Vasari is to be trusted) he worked in the Signorial Palace, studying Leonardo's cartoons and frescos, and learning from them nuances of chiaroscuro and color. But it was the Sistine that most impressed him, and led him to aim at more monumental effects, approximating more closely to sculpture. In his *Charity* at the Louvre we are struck by the abstract quality he has imparted to the forms, both by enclosing the whole group within a geometrical figure and also by a very special use of color.

"An exquisitely sensitive personality but without real depth"—thus has been described this artist whose talent was obviously greater than his creative power. He was perhaps overmuch dazzled by the greatness of some of his contemporaries, and found it hard to discover for himself new forms of art springing from that dark compulsion which lies at the heart of genius. And it is doubtless in such of his pictures as called for less elaborate effects, for example the *Portrait of a Sculptor* (London) and the *Portrait of his Wife* (Madrid), and also in his drawings, that Andrea del Sarto seems most at ease, most natural, and reveals his sensitive talent at its best. This portrait of Lucrezia, his wife, is set in, so to speak, a minor key, and the painter's inspiration is freely rendered in a vibrant harmony of tones. The chiaroscuro gradually dies away into the dark background, and the faintly misted colors, in a fawn-hued ambiance, set up overtones which call forth charming echoes in Lucrezia's hazel eyes, evoking new harmonics. True, here, too, there are traces of the influence of Leonardo; nevertheless Andrea del Sarto has imbued his wife's likeness with so rare and delicate a charm that in this portrait the personality of a highly strung, sensitive artist makes itself characteristically and exquisitely felt.

ANDREA DEL SARTO (1486-1530). PORTRAIT OF THE ARTIST'S WIFE, LUCREZIA (DETAIL). PRADO, MADRID.

INTERIOR OF SISTINE CHAPEL. VATICAN PALACE.

FRESCOS OF MICHELANGELO
IN THE SISTINE CHAPEL

The following pages contain the most significant and characteristic of Michelangelo's frescos on the ceiling of the Sistine Chapel. We believe this to be the first time these works have been reproduced from blocks engraved on the basis of direct color-separations. The direct color-separation process— i.e. photographic separation of the colors carried out on the spot—involved problems of an extremely delicate nature, but all, in spite of innumerable difficulties, have been successfully overcome.

To ensure success it was necessary to employ the most perfected instruments and, on occasion, to have recourse to entirely new methods.

The plan of using scaffolding had to be abandoned, since to ensure the complete immobility essential for successively registering the different colors, it would have been necessary to steady the scaffolding by making it abut on the side walls of the Chapel; and this would have endangered the frescos on them, which are as fragile as they are precious.

By using apparatus specially built for the purpose, we have succeeded in registering with absolute precision and fidelity the nuances of the tones and the exact texture of the surface of these frescos, which owing to their height above the ground, and given the ordinary lighting of the Chapel, are hardly perceptible to the naked eye.

It is due to the great kindness of the high ecclesiastical and civil authorities of the Vatican City that we have been able to carry out this work, and it is a pleasure to record our profound gratitude to them, which will be shared, we do not doubt, by all who thanks to these reproductions can now form an exact idea of this masterpiece by Michelangelo, one of the most sublime achievements of human genius.

PHOTOGRAPHY BY HANS HINZ, BASEL
ASSISTED BY M. BIEDER, ZURICH

ALL RIGHTS OF REPRODUCTION RESERVED
COPYRIGHT BY EDITIONS D'ART ALBERT SKIRA, GENEVA (SWITZERLAND)

MICHELANGELO (1475-1564). CEILING, SISTINE CHAPEL. JESSE (DETAIL). VATICAN PALACE.

—   —

MICHELANGELO (1475-1564). CEILING, SISTINE CHAPEL. THE CREATION OF ADAM (DETAIL). VATICAN PALACE.

MICHELANGELO

Against the crowded background of the sixteenth century Michelangelo looms large, a tragic, Promethean figure, gifted with perhaps the most gigantic creative force that the world has known. And if ever artist 'saw big,' it was he; always at grips with reality, he could capture it only by magnifying it, making it larger than life. And in his writings, in eyewitness accounts, in chronicles of the period, are recorded the trials and triumphs of a genius that could never make its peace with the world.

Michelangelo was born in 1475 at Caprese, a small town in the Casentino, where his father, Ludovico Buonarroti, was the mayor. As a young boy he was apprenticed to Ghirlandaio, but, apart from some technical procedures, he learnt little from this master, whose placid, illustrative art followed an already outmoded Quattrocento tradition. His natural bent was towards sculpture, and he owed the real start of his career to Lorenzo de' Medici, who took him into his household and, from 1489 to 1492, brought him up with his sons. Thus in the famous Medici 'Garden School' at the Piazza di San Marco he could feast his eyes on all the treasures of ancient and contemporary art. But Lorenzo's death abruptly shattered the tranquillity he had so far enjoyed, and when Piero de' Medici came to power, Michelangelo, foreseeing perhaps the impending fall of the Medici, moved to Venice and then to Bologna. At the last-named town, where he completed the carvings on St Dominic's sarcophagus, he became acquainted with the sculpture of Jacopo della Quercia. Soon after returning to Florence he set off for Rome and while there made, amongst other works of sculpture, a *Bacchus*, actually a rather frigid, conventional production inspired by classical Antiquity, and a *Pietà*, a group composition, in which he chiefly aimed at tender grace and harmony. Returning to Florence, he started work on the famous statue of *David* which he

MICHELANGELO (1475-1564). CEILING, SISTINE CHAPEL. THE DRUNKENNESS OF NOAH (DETAIL). VATICAN PALACE.

completed in less than four years, using an immense block of granite which had stood idle for years in the Cathedral workyard. The difficulties he had to overcome, owing to the dimensions of the block, stimulated Michelangelo's zeal; at last he had an opportunity of showing decisively the stuff he was made of. And he was completely successful; this unheard-of *tour de force* filled the Florentines with wonder and with admiration of the handsome peasant lad, whose commanding presence impressed them hardly less than this proof of his abilities. After much discussion they installed the statue in the Loggia of the Signorial Palace. Now that his reputation was made as a leading artist of the day, Michelangelo received many commissions, amongst them being the task of painting one wall of the great council chamber in the City Hall where Leonardo now was working. But this fresco was never made. Regarding sculpture as the supreme art, Michelangelo held that "the nearer painting comes to sculpture the more beautiful it is." In his cartoon for the fresco he showed a group of naked soldiers; he wished to demonstrate both the effectiveness of his plastic technique and his skill in rendering bodies in movement. And this work, no less than Leonardo's, had far-reaching effects on all subsequent art.

In 1505 Michelangelo was summoned to Rome; and now began that protracted 'tragedy of the tomb' (as the artist himself described it) which was to last until his death. When planning the new basilica of St Peter's, Pope Julius II decided to have his tomb placed in the apse, and he commissioned Michelangelo to take charge of the work. The sculptor himself went to the quarries of Carrara to select his marble, and stayed there eight months, sometimes lost in happy visions of the supreme works that he would call forth from these huge blocks of stone, sometimes fretting at the attitude of the quarrymen and the practical difficulties he foresaw. On returning to Rome he found that the Pope, at the instigation perhaps of Bramante and others of his ill-wishers, had given up the project for the tomb, and now wished Michelangelo to paint the ceiling of the Sistine Chapel. Disgusted by this notion, even, it would seem, panic-stricken—so abrupt was his decision to leave Rome—Michelangelo hastened back to Florence (1506).

Two years later, however, yielding to the threats and entreaties of Pope Julius, he started work on the fresco, though inwardly he loathed the task as much as ever. He began by getting rid of his assistants; then continued working, unaided and under constant pressure from the Pope, for the next four years. The surface to be painted was a rectangle measuring approximately 44 by 15 yards. The original design of the fresco, which comprised only geometrical figures and representations of the twelve Apostles, was entirely remade and given an elaborate setting. The structural layout simulates architectural divisions in which are ensconced statuary figures; it is divided into three long tracts of ceiling, intersected by nine transverse sections, in which figure scenes from the Book of Genesis—the general impression being that of an architectural roof in which nine pictures are embedded. Its effect on those who see it for the first time is one of bewildering vastness, of a hardly bearable tension, a direct assault on the imagination. The splendid bodies of the *ignudi* (the name given by the painter's contemporary, Condivi, to the nudes in the four corners of the central panel), the monumental drapery that billows round the brooding silence of the prophets, those hauntingly beautiful figures of the Sibyls with their air of wondering ecstasy—all combine to give this monstrous world, teeming with elemental life, an aspect of fatality; as though these giants, conjured up from the void, were bound by a doom putting them outside the pale of the human. It has been said that here we have a reflection of the painter's state of mind; yet airless, overcrowded as it is, this huge composition expresses more than an individual predicament, it also symbolizes the moral, religious, and metaphysical chaos of this phase of the Renaissance.

Conscious of the cleavage that was now developing between Man and the world around him, Leonardo assigned to atmosphere the creative role and steeped his figures in the glimmering vastness of air and sky; Michelangelo, the sculptor born, glorifies physical beauty and creates supermen, whose greatness is no longer in keeping with a world which God is now abandoning.

True, Savonarola's tirades against the decay of the religious sentiment had made a deep impression on Michelangelo, but they had done nothing to restore a vital relation between Man and God. Thus the God on the Sistine ceiling is essentially a supernatural being; there is less benevolence in Him than power, and He is not so much a creator of human life as an arbiter of doom.

We can easily picture the admiration of contemporaries and the influence of this gigantic vision on later generations. This glorification of volumes instinct with movement, boldly foreshortened or emphasizing the contrast between their hugeness and the smallness of the space into which they are compressed, came as a new revelation of the sovereign power of art. Yet, in one way, this art merely implemented a plastic tradition familiar to the Quattrocento. Unlike the art of Leonardo, whose discoveries opened up new vistas to painting, Michelangelo's was self-contained, complete in itself. And thus, though it was often reproduced as a procedure, it rarely served as a source of new inspiration; its plastic treatment of figures soon became an academic formula, and the movement Michelangelo had imparted to them soon became mere attitudes, devoid of real meaning.

Pope Julius' death in 1513 brought the problem of the tomb, which actually had only just been begun, to a head. Bit by bit the original plan, now seen to be over-ambitious, was whittled down by a series of new contracts; so things went on until 1544, and finally the building of the tomb was put into the hands of others. Only the *Moses* and two statues, emblems of the Active and the Contemplative Life respectively, were completed by Michelangelo himself. During the long years when this constantly frustrated project for the tomb

MICHELANGELO (1475-1564). CEILING, SISTINE CHAPEL. THE PROPHET JONAH. VATICAN PALACE.

MICHELANGELO (1475-1564). CEILING, SISTINE CHAPEL. THE PROPHET JEREMIAH
(DETAIL). VATICAN PALACE.

weighe   ever on his mind, Michelangelo was often blamed for his dilatoriness and even
accusec of having wantonly failed to do work for which he had been paid. Actually the
delay v is largely due to the amount of other work demanded of him. In 1516 Leo X
asked h n to decorate the façade of the church of San Lorenzo; in 1521 the Pope gave
him an   rder for the mortuary chapel of the Medici in this church, and the contract was
renewed)y his successor Clement VII, who also had him complete the Lorenzo de' Medici
Library egun in 1524.

Afte   the sack of Rome in 1527 Michelangelo moved to Florence, but at the fall of
the Medi   he suddenly fled to Venice (1529)—an act which brought him under suspicion
with a certain section of the Florentines. He had thought of going to France, but changed
his mind and until 1534, when he settled in Rome for good, divided his time between the two
cities, busy continuously with work on the Medici mansion, commissioned by the Pope.

MICHELANGELO (1475-1564). CEILING, SISTINE CHAPEL. THE DELPHIC SIBYL (DETAIL). VATICAN PALACE.

Clement VII died two days after Michelangelo's coming to Rome, and Paul III ordered the artist to cover the wall behind the altar in the Sistine Chapel with a fresco—a project Clement VII had had in mind and in view of which Michelangelo had made several preliminary sketches. But he did not actually start work on the *Last Judgement* until 1534.

When, in 1541, the fresco was unveiled, the public was genuinely shocked by this apocalyptic scene, the seething mass of naked bodies racked by the agonies of the damned, by torments mental and physical, on whom Christ launched the thunderbold of His divine vengeance, pouring the vials of His wrath on all alike, the blessed and the damned. The sight of these tangled masses of nudes caused nothing short of a scandal, there was talk of *terribilità*, and Aretino who had vainly tried to have his version of the *Last Judgement* accepted was amongst Michelangelo's bitterest opponents. As a result, soon after the 'release' of the work, the nudes were covered with drapery. This fresco is now in poor condition, and it is hard to tell how the colors originally looked—though, according to Vasari, the scene never had any 'grace of color.' Still we cannot but be impressed by the stupendous tragic force which has thus distorted the volumes of bodies, destroying and remolding them, the uncontrolled expression of a mighty genius. As far as painting was concerned, this *Last Judgement* was intended by Michelangelo to be his last work. Asked in 1542 to paint the Paolina Chapel at the Vatican, he consented reluctantly; apart from the fact that he had never been much drawn to painting, he felt too old to undertake such a task. And, in fact, these frescos show signs of weariness; it would seem that he had said his last word, and the driving force of his rebellious spirit had spent itself in the *Last Judgement*. His last work was the so-called 'Rondanini' *Pietà* which, unfinished though it is, may be regarded as the final cadence of that vast symphony of the creative spirit and constructive form embodied in the life's work of this titanic yet profoundly human artist.

MICHELANGELO (1475-1564). CEILING, SISTINE CHAPEL. THE PROPHET DANIEL. VATICAN PALACE.

MICHELANGELO (1475-1564). CEILING, SISTINE CHAPEL. THE FALL OF MAN (DETAIL). VATICAN PALACE.

MICHELANGELO (1475-1564). CEILING, SISTINE CHAPEL. THE PROPHET DANIEL (DETAIL). VATICAN PALACE.

MICHELANGELO (1475-1564). CEILING, SISTINE CHAPEL. THE STORY OF ESTHER (DETAIL). VATICAN PALACE.

MICHELANGELO (1475-1564). CEILING, SISTINE CHAPEL. JUDITH AND HOLOPHERNES (DETAIL). VATICAN PALACE.

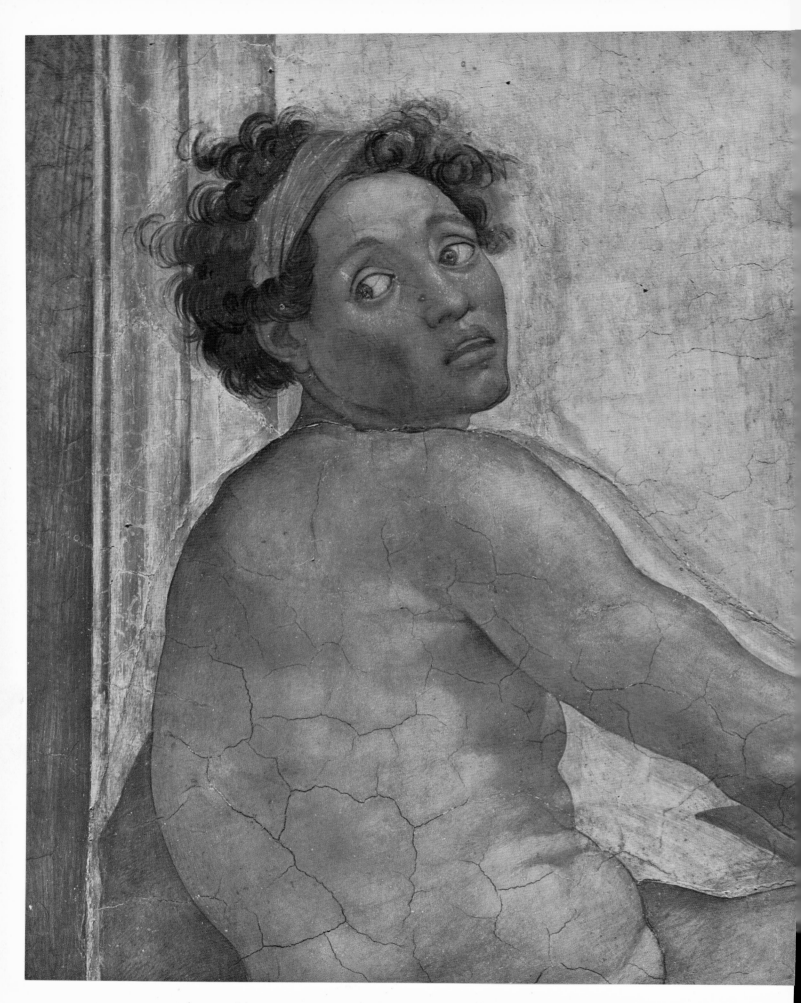

MICHELANGELO (1475-1564). CEILING, SISTINE CHAPEL. DECORATIVE FIGURE (DETAIL). VATICAN PALACE.

MICHELANGELO (1475-1564). CEILING, SISTINE CHAPEL. DECORATIVE FIGURE (DETAIL). VATICAN PALACE.

MICHELANGELO (1475-1564). CEILING, SISTINE CHAPEL. THE FALL OF MAN (DETAIL). VATICAN PALACE.

MICHELANGELO (1475-1564). CEILING, SISTINE CHAPEL. THE CREATION OF EVE (DETAIL). VATICAN PALACE.

MICHELANGELO (1475-1564). CEILING, SISTINE CHAPEL. DECORATIVE FIGURE. VATICAN PALACE.

MICHELANGELO (1475-1564). CEILING, SISTINE CHAPEL. DECORATIVE FIGURE. VATICAN PALACE.

MICHELANGELO (1475-1564). THE ENTOMBMENT. (62½×58½") NATIONAL GALLERY, LONDON.
REPRODUCED BY COURTESY OF THE TRUSTEES

Though the figures in The Entombment *retain something of the grandiose arabesque of the Creation of the World—where form, in the sublimity of its power and its sweeping movement, took precedence of all else—we find in them a tendency to flex the line and override the movement, while the bodies are distorted as though some inner fire were coursing through them, actuating their dancing rhythm.*

At that time many painters aimed at giving form alone the function of re-creating life; but this program was far from being universally endorsed in the divided Italy of the second half of the Cinquecento. From this conflict of ideas was to arise the art of the Mannerists.

PONTORMO AND BRONZINO

Pontormo belongs to that generation of Florentine painters which spanned the first half of the sixteenth century. Exceptionally gifted, he seemed to have all the makings of a first-rank painter. But his art never came into its own, stunted as it were, by the pressure of an ever more insistent will to formal expression. Sensitive, perhaps hypersensitive, he could never rise above himself and his inner conflicts and create with the detachment so essential to the artist. In fact his career is a striking illustration of the decline of the vital impulse that, at the beginning of the Cinquecento, made itself so lamentably felt in Florence. He takes his place in the school of painters whom we call, after an Italian word, 'mannerist,' and who brought to its close a whole Platonic, intellectual tradition peculiar to Florence. The painters grouped together under that somewhat vague appellation 'Mannerists,' were very numerous at this time and highly thought of. Moreover, they enjoyed the favor of the greatest in the land; thus Pontormo and Bronzino supplied paintings to the Medici court, Beccafumi worked for the Republic of Siena, and Rosso was summoned to France, to the court of Francis I. But after their deaths, for many centuries, they were almost completely forgotten. In any case Vasari had expressed only a qualified admiration for this kind of art; he accused them of being too prone to "complicate their form." It was left to modern art critics to rescue them from undeserved oblivion; thus it is now recognized that they genuinely tried to strike out in new directions and did not merely turn out imitations of the past, soulless, devoid of content, as was once supposed.

Pontormo was born in 1494. His real name was Jacopo Carrucci, but he took the name of his birthplace, a village near Empoli, in Tuscany. If we can trust Vasari, Pontormo first studied under Leonardo, then under Piero di Cosimo, and lastly under Andrea del Sarto. We have no other record of this, but it is probable enough that the young painter, restless by nature, should have gone from teacher to teacher in quest of a congenial means of expression.

It was in 1513, for the façade of the Church of La Santa Annunziata at Florence, that he painted his first important work, now lost. His contemporaries were wildly enthusiastic in their praises of the young artist, and Vasari quotes Michelangelo as saying at the time: "If he lives and continues on this path, Pontormo will carry painting to heavenly heights." And as a result of this success Pontormo's name was made.

Towards 1520 he took part in decorating the Villa Poggio a Caiano, where Andrea del Sarto was already at work. Around the windows, under the vaulting, he depicted the myth of Pomona and Vertumnus, a work at once harmonious and full of poetic feeling. The composition is freely built up within the limits set by the architecture; figures and countryside are treated in a decorative style that brings to mind the illustrations of a fairy-tale. Though we have echoes of Michelangelo in the full, bold modeling of the figures, Pontormo does not seek to conjure up a transcendental world. On the contrary, he is careful to strike a balance between decorative form and directly psychological interpretation, 'anti-intellectual' as it has been called, and nearer to reality.

In 1522, fleeing the plague, he left Florence and painted the narrative of the *Passion* in the cloister of the Carthusian monastery of the Val d'Ema. His art now underwent a change which became more and more pronounced as time went on. His forms lenghten out, the figures become contorted, as if writhing in the throes of utter despair, with the eyes dilated, and in strained, strongly emotive attitudes. The intricate lay-out of the bodies and the cold, acid tones employed in his *Deposition* (in the Church of Santa Felicita at Florence) illustrate the need he now felt for expression stepped-up to its maximum intensity. Vasari criticized this change and attributed it to an excessive fondness on Pontormo's part for German painting, for Dürer in particular. There may be some truth in this; yet the influence of Michelangelo remains no less obvious. For ever restless and dissatisfied, Pontormo sought more and more after forms expressive of all that supersedes reality. But too impressionable, too much at

PONTORMO (1494-1556). PORTRAIT OF A LADY. (35 × 27½″) STAEDELSCHES INSTITUT, FRANKFORT.

the mercy of his nerves, he could never rise above the expression of an almost frenzied agitation, and even in many of his portraits we find this same excited handling of form. To be sure, when he has to portray real people, his habit of distortion is kept under more control. But even so his people always seem to be denizens of some far-away, melancholy world, summoned forth from it against their will. In 1546 Pontormo started on a series of frescos for the choir of the Church of San Lorenzo. These he had not quite finished when he died in 1556, on the last day of the year. This work brought his life to its close on a tragic note, for his contemporaries did not stint their criticism. Thus Borghini wrote: "He has made a mountain of fat bodies... and it is a very ugly sight."

ANGELO BRONZINO (1503-1572). PORTRAIT OF ELEONORA OF TOLEDO AND HER SON JOHN.
(45×37½″) PITTI PALACE, FLORENCE.

When his *Last Judgment* was shown to the public, Michelangelo, too, came in for bitter attacks. And Pontormo shocked a public that could not see beyond the morbid side of his work and its extreme distortion of forms. If the supposition that the artist ended by embracing the doctrines of the Italian Reformation be correct, there is aptness in the observation that "seen in this light, this cycle of frescos can be regarded as a dialogue between Pontormo and death and the life of the soul after death."

Bronzino was not only Pontormo's pupil, but also the friend and disciple who worked at his side for many years. Born in 1503, dead in 1572, he too belongs to that phase of art called 'Mannerism,' which for so long has been looked on as the decadence of Cinquecento art, and a mere rehash of old procedures. Actually this was a transitional period and as such involving new departures. True, such painters as Pontormo and Bronzino never rose to real greatness. But their very shortcomings enable us to trace the transition from the defunctive Cinquecento art-world to that born of the Reformation and the Counter-Reformation.

Bronzino's output was abundant. In 1523 he worked with Pontormo at the Carthusian monastery of the Val d'Ema, and painted single-handed the frescos of the *Pietà* and the *Martyrdom of St Lawrence*. In 1530 he took work in the service of the Duke of Urbino. Back in Florence, he spent most of his time doing portraits, but also turned his hand to painting some of Pontormo's cartoons for the Villa Careggi, as well as working under his master's direction at the Villa di Castello. In 1540 the Duke of Como engaged him as court painter and in 1545 an important commission came his way when he was asked to decorate Duchess Eleonora's private chapel in the Palazzo della Signoria. He worked on this until some time after 1564. In his religious and allegorical works Bronzino took great liberties with the spirit of the subjects. His concern was with a pure representation of forms, treated in a rhythm increasingly complex, with special emphasis on physical beauty.

Despite his cult of form for its own sake, Pontormo always imparted to it something of his own unquiet temperament. Bronzino, on the other hand, accustomed to moving in court circles, had but one thing in mind: the greatest possible intellectual refinement and elegance of style. Religious themes were ill-suited to such a temperament and his output is, in fact, entirely academic in nature.

Portraiture was a medium better suited to his personality. Faced by a human being, Bronzino sought to escape from the realities of his subject by a meticulous, sometimes over-copious treatment of details and extreme *finesse* of execution. His people are like manne-quins or abstract beings, distinguishable one from the other chiefly by the signs of their relative affluence and social position. He was debarred from rendering individual character, since doing this would have meant impairing what he regarded as the perfection of the human form. Thus when he portrays a sculptor, he tries to suggest the personality of his sitter by painting in a statuette beside him. In another picture the clue consists of archi-tecture in the background, or a bird held in a child's hands. By sidestepping immediate reality, he often ends up in a form of realism ('verismo'). Yet, though severely formal, the precision of his art lends an air of haughtiness and nobility to his portraits; we feel these people are the last survivors of an aristocratic world, tottering to its fall.

TOWARDS AN IDEAL BEAUTY

RAPHAEL

RAPHAEL (1483-1520). ST CECILIA, ALTARPIECE OF ST CECILIA (DETAIL). PINACOTECA NAZIONALE, BOLOGNA.

RAPHAEL

While we may picture Leonardo's long life as a whirl of undertakings entered into and but partially fulfilled, harried by a creative impulse that aimed at nothing short of miracles, Raphael's career was very different, serene and uniformly happy, for he advanced from triumph to triumph until his death.

Raphael (Raffaello Sanzio) was born, in 1483, at Urbino, which, thanks to the efforts of the Duke Federico da Montefeltro, had become a flourishing center of art and culture. Whereas Leonardo in his feverish quest of movement had shattered the limitations of Quattrocento art and introduced chiaroscuro into space; and whereas Michelangelo had boldly flung himself into a Promethean struggle between man and the universe, Raphael gave the world an art of smiling grace, of balanced power, of sensitive yet broadly flowing lines, inspired by the forms of Antiquity and invigorated by a calm but profound feeling for an ideal, flawless beauty.

The surroundings of his childhood and his early contacts with art had a lasting effect on his temperament. There was little of the revolutionary about him, and the pleasant atmosphere of his hometown favored the natural sweetness of his disposition. Duke Federico, who died a year before the painter's birth, had done much for the amenities of Raphael's birthplace; the Ducal Palace, planned by the architect Luciano Laurana, was not only an edifice of fine proportions and a very real beauty, but contained one of the best stocked libraries of the period, elegant sculptures, as well as paintings by Melozzo da Forli, and works by Signorelli and the Fleming Justus of Ghent. But it was Piero della Francesca, a friend and protégé of the Duke, who had contributed above all to the artistic ambiance of the Palace, with his constructive rhythms and sense of design, the gentle radiance of his light and color.

When Raphael was only eleven his father, Giovanni Santi (who was a painter) died; but not before he had given his little son a very real taste for art, and introduced him to the leading literary men and artists of Urbino. A great admirer of Perugino, he naturally pointed Raphael's way towards his teacher-to-be. It was in or about the year 1500 that Raphael started to learn his craft from Perugino, who was then at the splendid zenith of his powers, aged about fifty-five, snowed under with orders for pictures, and assisted in his work by several pupils. Raphael was much struck by the distinctive excellences of his master's painting: well-balanced composition without any crowding of details, an unsophisticated joy in nature, sincere religious feeling, a shade conventional perhaps, but tinged with poetry and rarely lacking a warm human appeal, if sometimes lyrically idealized. Moreover it was in Perugino's studio that young Raphael gleaned his first impressions of what was going on in the art-world of contemporary Florence.

Of his output during this early phase, in which the influence of his teacher is always more or less perceptible, it is the smaller pictures rather than the altarpieces that display the elegant design, the grace and freshness of inspiration that characterize Raphael's art at this stage of his career. *The Vision of a Knight*, for instance, is a poetic fairy story told in a deliberately simple way, in warm tonalities and with a very taking rhythm.

His youthful contacts with the Court of Urbino had given Raphael a happy capacity for appreciating all forms of art. Thus, having heard others speak with enthusiasm and admiration of the wonderful work being done in Florence by Leonardo and Michelangelo, he "threw up what he was then engaged on and, giving no thought to personal convenience or practical considerations, he moved to Florence"—thus Vasari. He stayed four years in Florence, from 1504 to 1508, working with immense zeal, trying his hand at transcribing the new forms of his contemporaries but also studying closely the art of Antiquity.

Raphael's output during this period was immense. Time and again he painted the "Madonna and Child," a theme for which all his life long he had a predilection and which, as rendered by him, has never lost its popular appeal. The color which, in a very delicate

RAPHAEL (1483-1520). ST GEORGE AND THE DRAGON. (12½ × 10½″) LOUVRE, PARIS.

chiaroscuro, so elegantly marks the transitions from light to shade, the broad, free drawing, and above all a natural skill in building up the composition which, interpreting and adjusting the procedures of Leonardo and Michelangelo, gives constructive solidity to the whole—these qualities explain and justify the high esteem these pictures have enjoyed in many lands and ages. Nevertheless, it is not in his Madonnas that Raphael best displays his rare gift for exploring the secret places of the human soul; nor do we find in them the expression of a deep religious feeling. When we recall that first 'holy conversation' (to give the scene its Italian name) painted by Pietro Lorenzetti in the Church of Assisi, we realize what Raphael's age had lost in mystical depth, and how persistently the 'profane' was encroaching on the 'holy' in religious art. Thus the Madonna, idealized no longer in an uprush of mystical emotion but with an eye to an ideal beauty, was by way of becoming almost an abstract, if supremely lovely figure—beauty incarnate, devoid of any human feeling.

It is in his portraits that we see Raphael's gift for characterization given its most powerful expression. Usually there is an abstract background, dark or luminous, and the figure tells out against it: a sudden, utterly convincing presence, simplified by the idealization of its personal traits. For Raphael's psychological power reveals itself not in nuances of character but in his gift of causing the portrait to make its full effect *qua* picture.

RAPHAEL (1483-1520). VISION OF A KNIGHT. (6½ × 6½″) NATIONAL GALLERY, LONDON.
REPRODUCED BY COURTESY OF THE TRUSTEES

85

RAPHAEL (1483-1520). ST CATHERINE OF ALEXANDRIA (DETAIL). NATIONAL GALLERY, LONDON.
REPRODUCED BY COURTESY OF THE TRUSTEES

During his stay in Florence the young painter's renown steadily increased. A letter of his to his uncle (1508) gives news of his activities in Florence, his hopes of getting commissions for France, and his contacts with Rome. So as to escape the daily sight of the portrait of his detested predecessor (Alexander VI), Pope Julius II decided to leave the Borgia mansion, and in 1508 engaged a group of painters—Sodoma, Bramantino, Lotto, Peruzzi— to decorate his new residence. Shortly after, probably on the advice of Bramante and the Urbino Court, he called in Raphael, and before long put him in entire charge of the work. The Pope's decree to this effect, dated 1509, is the first written record we have of the artist's presence in Rome.

For the first time Raphael was confronted with large surfaces to be treated; also the artistic climate in Rome was very different from what he had been used to hitherto. Moreover, though he had a good many years' experience behind him he was still quite young, only twenty-six.

The great fresco of *The School of Athens* in the Stanza della Segnatura is dated 1511. The broadness of the composition, the rhythmical distribution of the space it occupies, the arrangement of the architectural elements, and the stately recession of the central arches give this work a monumental grandeur, often described as classical. Actually the painter had not in mind a literal restatement of any of the principles of Antiquity; the sense of dignity emanating from this picture is due to the all-pervading unity of the composition, the perfect balance of all the parts. There is something almost theatrical in the arrangement of the groups and the attitudes of the individual figures. And this feeling for stage effects, associated with the majestic sweep and freedom of the lay-out as a whole, is deeply impressive, we have here an almost unique fusion of a superb ideal with its visual realization.

Beauty self-sufficient, existing in its own right without any ulterior consideration, was Raphael's aim. Nevertheless his greater works are full of poetic feeling, a shining purity; and, moreover, the bodies are *real* bodies, not projections of ideal forms. A passage in a letter (addressed to Baldassare Castiglione) generally thought to have been written by Raphael, and often quoted, runs as follows: "I would have you know that to paint a picture of a beautiful woman, I would really need to see several beautiful women and have to make it a condition that Your Lordship helped me to select the best. But as there is a scarcity of good judges and beautiful women, I have to make do with the ideas that cross my mind."

Even in *The School of Athens* Raphael aims at creating beauty; though the persons figuring in it, "eager to teach or to be taught," are intended to illustrate the fellowship of the philosophers, the true function of each and all is to body forth physical beauty in their various attitudes, sublimated by the ideal animating them. True, it is a 'manifesto' of culture in one sense; but it is transfigured into a vision of beauty by the deep poetic feeling of the artist.

The famous portrait of a Cardinal in the Prado, Madrid, belongs approximately to the same period. This is regarded as one of the peak-points of Raphael's art and in it he achieves a perfect fusion of character-expression and idealization. All attempts to identify the sitter for this portrait have failed; yet we have a curious feeling that this is someone we have always known. "He is nothing more or less," Ortolani wrote, "than archetypal man, at once all character and all lyrical abstraction." Notable here is the richness and intensity Raphael has imparted to the cardinalian scarlet. It is no mere block of inert color; the red comes to glowing life in the constant transitions from plane to plane. And its contrast with the translucent, delicate pallor of the face imparts to this portrait an amazing grandeur. Yet here there are no clashes of tonalities, no broken rhythms; all is perfectly balanced, unified by the idealized handling of the lines and the skilfully disposed recalls of the colors. The dignity of this portrait does not stem from the expression on the sitter's face or from the attributes of his high rank, but from the aristocratic quality of the painting, as painting.

The fresco of the *Mass of Bolsena* bears the date 1512. A change has occurred between the *School of Athens* and this picture; the pale, chalky tones which Raphael used in the former have given place to warm, richly glowing tones. Probably the painter had meanwhile

RAPHAEL (1483-1520). PORTRAIT OF ANGELO DONI (DETAIL). PITTI PALACE, FLORENCE.

RAPHAEL (1483-1520). PORTRAIT OF A CARDINAL (DETAIL). PRADO, MADRID.

RAPHAEL (1483-1520). PLATO AND ARISTOTLE, THE SCHOOL OF ATHENS (DETAIL). FRESCO.
STANZA DELLA SEGNATURA, VATICAN PALACE.

seen something of the Venetian handling of color, perhaps in the work of Sebastiano del Piombo who was working in Rome at the time. But the intensity of the color, especially in the group of kneeling Swiss soldiers on the right of the picture, has nothing derivative about it and its strongly emotive effect bespeaks the genius of Raphael alone. He seems to wish

RAPHAEL (1483-1520). GROUP OF SWISS SOLDIERS, THE MASS OF BOLSENA (DETAIL). STANZA DI ELIODORO, VATICAN PALACE.

to bring out the exact texture of each object; the loaded, muffled colors of the costumes contrast with the grey of the marble and the cool tints of the faces. The clean-cut drawing, precisely fixing expressions with a simplification that is clearly intentional, gives this group a striking quality of 'actuality.'

The decoration of the Stanze had created a great stir; and as might be expected in an age where art was a burning topic of the day, two parties entered the lists: Raphael's champions and Michelangelo's defenders, the result being a spate of passionate controversies. Actually Michelangelo's treatment of the Sistine ceiling had repercussions on Raphael's art; this influence is particularly apparent in his *Fire of Borgo*, where he aimed at sculptural effects. However the result was not particularly happy; such procedures were ill-suited to Raphael's artistic personality.

When Julius II died, his successor Leo X appointed (in 1514) Raphael, as a temporary measure, architect of St Peter's in Bramante's stead. A letter from Raphael to his uncle gives some details of his reactions to this new task assigned him. "In any case I am compelled to stay in Rome because of the building operations at St Peter's, in respect of which I have taken over from Bramante. But what city in the world is greater than Rome, and what edifice greater than St Peter's? It is the chief temple of the world, the biggest building that has ever been seen, it is going to cost over a million in gold, and let me tell you, the Pope is determined to spend sixty thousand ducats on it during the present year, and can think of nothing else." The feeling that he was living in a supremely exciting age, teeming with grandiose conceptions, and his unfailing interest in all cultural developments explain Raphael's readiness to join in every undertaking that caught his fancy, even if it meant a dispersal of his creative powers. Thus, besides easel paintings, the decoration of the Stanze at the Vatican, the picture of the *Elephant* given to the Pope by the King of Portugal, he undertook the task of making cartoons for the tapestries which, woven in Flanders, were to adorn the Sistine Chapel. Exhibited in 1519, "these seven panels are esteemed the best thing of the kind that has ever been done, and this despite the great renown of the tapestries owned by the Marquess of Mantua, made after designs by Mantegna," a contemporary writes.

In 1518 Raphael was still engaged in decorating the Farnesina, the summer residence of the family of the wealthy banker Chigi, a warm admirer of the artist. In this vast *ensemble* dealing with non-religious themes, a good deal of the work was done by Raphael's assistants; even in the *Galatea* fresco, which Raphael is known to have painted single-handed, we seem to have an attempt, conscious rather than spontaneous, to recapture the forms of Antiquity as the people of his day supposed them to have been.

It is not only his paintings that bring home to us Raphael's interest in classical Antiquity; it is also illustrated by various incidents mentioned in the records of the time. Thus when in 1515 he was authorized by the Pope to purchase marbles and "antique stones" for the *fabbrica* of St Peter's, he noted down the ancient inscriptions on them. In 1518 Leo X appointed him, together with Antonio di San Gallo, 'Superintendant of the Streets of Rome,' in other words he was responsible for the lay-out and good order of the city. And, bearing the next year's date, is a letter to the Pope deploring the wretched state of many of the old buildings, and suggesting that a plan of Rome should be drawn up, based on the texts of the classical writers, and giving precise, graphic delineations of the monuments and edifices of ancient Rome. It is probable, though not absolutely certain, that Raphael was the writer of this letter. If he was, it is another proof of the high esteem in which he held classical Antiquity—an esteem not of course peculiar to himself, but in keeping with the general outlook of the men of the Renaissance.

The decorations of the Farnesina were a signal for renewed attacks on Raphael by some of Michelangelo's supporters. Thus Leonardo Sellaio, in a letter dated 1518 to Michelangelo wrote: "Agostino Chigi's ceiling has now been uncovered; these decorations are a disgrace to a great master." And Sebastiano del Piombo, who painted a *Resurrection of Lazarus* to vie with Raphael's *Transfiguration*, wrote (also to Michelangelo): "I am sorry you were not in Rome to see the two pictures (by Raphael) which have just left for France;

RAPHAEL (1483-1520). SWISS SOLDIER, THE MASS OF BOLSENA (DETAIL).
FRESCO, STANZA DI ELIODORO, VATICAN PALACE.

you could not imagine, I should say, anything more contrary to your taste than what these pictures would have shown you." Yet, apart from some hostile criticism of this order, Raphael was universally regarded as a painter of transcendent genius and when, in 1520, after being struck down by a raging fever, he died, on April 6, aged barely thirty-seven, the news of his death "caused vast distress, but especially amongst the men of learning," and indeed amongst the public too there was "universal lamentation, as if a god had passed away."

CORREGGIO (?1489-1534). STUDY FOR A NATIVITY. (10 × 7¼″) RED CHALK. LOUVRE, PARIS.

CORREGGIO

AND

PARMIGIANINO

P.I. 2 — 52

—   —

CORREGGIO (?1489-1534). MADONNA AND CHILD. (22½×17½″) GALLERIA D'ESTE, MODENA.

CORREGGIO

His discoveries in the fields of aerial perspective and atmospheric movement, of chiaroscuro and the gradual diminution of the luminosity of colors in recession, served Leonardo as means of expressing an ideal of an intellectual order. In the art of Correggio, however, his prodigious skill and a characteristically sensuous handling of light and color at once exalt and limit his art; indeed we may say that he treats as ends what Leonardo used as means.

Whereas Michelangelo created a world in which men and women had equal place upon a transcendental plane, Correggio devotes himself to an idealization of the beauty of women. He aims at bodying forth a special type of charm, almost impersonal in its presentation, in which forms are clad in a haze of broken gleams, expressions are always dignified and every attitude is one of supple grace.

With his soaring inspiration Raphael had lifted his religious scenes towards an ideal beauty far above earthbound reality. But there remains much that is sweetly and simply human in Correggio's Madonnas and Magdalens, even when transfigured by the alchemy of his art, and all about them tells of strange enchantments. And Correggio's influence was far-reaching; we feel its presence even after the eighteenth century.

The painter's real name was Antonio Allegri. There is no record of the exact date of his birth, but it is assumed to have taken place a little before 1489. And our information about his youth is even scantier. He died in 1534.

The small town of Correggio, whence he derived his name, was near Modena, and, like most townships of Cinquecento Italy, had its local court. A prominent figure there was Veronica Gambara, a lady of high intelligence and culture, who befriended the local artists, and gave them every encouragement. But though old-fashioned, provincial elements are obviously present in Correggio's art, he was no less obviously familiar with the innovations of his day; which suggests that he may have been in touch with the big art centers.

Probably Mantua was the scene of his initiation into art, and it was there he saw the works of Mantegna, and those of the Ferrara school, Lorenzo Costa's in particular. This last-named artist had recently replaced Mantegna, who died in 1506, at the Gonzaga court. Also, Correggio seems to have become acquainted with the art of Leonardo at an early age; but how and where there is no knowing. Nor have we any certain evidence of a journey he is believed to have made and in the course of which he saw the works of Michelangelo and Raphael. The truth is that it is his own works rather than contemporary records that tell us most of the influences he underwent and the path he chose in this early phase of his career. In or about 1519 he was summoned to Parma by the Abbess Giovanna Piacenza, to decorate a room at the S. Paolo convent. The theme of this fresco was of a 'pagan' order; it represents Diana with little attendant *putti*, genii of the chase, seen as if through windows, and in small lunettes along the cornice are allegorical subjects treated in monochrome. The painter had not yet quite found himself; for the general lay-out shows the influence of Mantegna amongst others, though the vivacity of movement and expression imparted to the small childish figures is distinctive, a foretaste of Correggio's later art.

But all the old traditions of the Quattrocento were now being reviewed in the light of Leonardo's art, and Correggio, always fascinated as he was by light effects, was quick to realize the possibilities open to him in this field, where Leonardo had been the pioneer. And by a skillful use of chiaroscuro and the fusion of forms in atmosphere he achieved those subtle effects of the play of light on colors and of forms freely moving in space which so enthrall us in his work. "Correggio," Stendhal writes, "combined forms more grandiose perhaps than Raphael's with a suavity and tenderness that no painter before him had achieved. He frankly wished to charm in every possible way... and even before appealing to the soul he wished his pictures to gratify the eye." This indeed is characteristic of Correggio's art; he is frankly out to charm, and we must admit that sometimes this leads to a certain

CORREGGIO (?1489-1534). ST JOHN AT PATMOS. FRESCO.
CHURCH OF S. GIOVANNI EVANGELISTA, PARMA.

affectation in the attitudes or, again, an overstressing of the coquetry of the movements of his figures. It is when the artist lets himself be guided wholly by his purely painterly instinct for vitality of color and the vibration of light that we see him at his best. He then creates a world whose gay, exquisitely chosen colors seem to radiate a sense of joy untrammelled, full of nobility and charm.

From 1520 onwards he was employed, again at Parma, on the decoration of the cupola of S. Giovanni Evangelista. "In the decoration of S. Giovanni," writes Adolfo Venturi, "we have the first demonstration of the possibilities of aerial perspective in painting a cupola: a demonstration which pointed the way to the art of the seventeenth century." It was, in fact, the first time composition of this kind had been attempted, illusion-painting of the boldest order, with strong foreshortenings, breaking through architecturally limited space and soaring heavenwards. Amidst billowing clouds Christ rises, and the foreshortened forms of the apostles arrayed in a circle round the cupola, act as a sort of foreground giving amplitude and emphasis to the spherical arrangement of the fresco. There is still some stiffness in the composition, and this imparts to it, as a whole, a sensation of repose, while the attitudes of the apostles are still determined by a feeling for the rhythmical distribution of masses. But when, in 1530, Correggio completed the decoration of the dome in the Cathedral at Parma, he gave free rein to movement of the boldest order; as though determined to show the magic power of art, the 'illusion-miracles' it can perform, he made of the *Assumption of the Virgin* a dizzying swirl of rising, concentric circles, formed by a ring of bodies caught up in the rhythms of an aerial dance. Baroque was near, the church was, so to speak, expanding, its vault becoming a playground for the clouds and skies alive with moving figures—a restless sort of place, which gave scant encouragement to prayerful meditation or indeed religious feeling of any serious order.

Correggio was full of the joy of living; and this is borne out by the suavity, charm and amiability of so many of his pictures. Though he began by using persistently a chiaroscuro of his own devising, in which the colors are brought out by glints of warmer tones, he subsequently practised a franker statement of form, a subtler use of tones, and a more mellow and sensuous rendering of light which, flooding bodies, seems to impart to them its characteristic vibrancy.

In his early phase, his constructive methods were still bound up with the traditions of the fifteenth century. But very soon he learnt to build up forms with the play of color and a skillful use of light and shade, and abolished the structural limitations of the canvas or the wall. In his work the transition from the old notions of painting to the new plastic vision took place in such a way that his art seems to link up directly with that of the seventeenth century, without passing through an intermediate stage of the classical style of the Cinquecento, as exemplified in Raphael.

CORREGGIO (?1489-1534). THE ASCENSION OF CHRIST. FRESCO.
CHURCH OF S. GIOVANNI EVANGELISTA, PARMA.

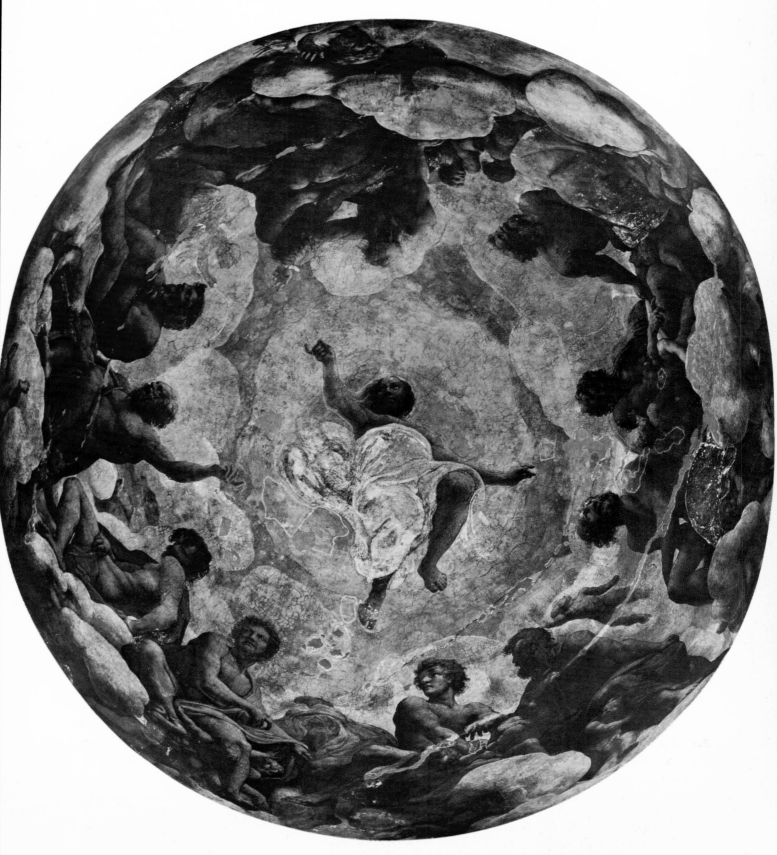

99

PARMIGIANINO

Correggio had built up compositions in which luminous colors imparted life to form and the bodies seemed to vibrate, light as motes in a sunbeam, in infinite space. Nevertheless owing to its frankly sensuous nature, Correggio's work came very close to life. Almost his contemporary, Francesco Mazzola was born in 1503 at Parma (whence the name Parmigianino by which he is generally known). Though his art stemmed directly from Correggio's, it matured into a quite different form of expression.

In 1522 Parmigianino was employed in S. Giovanni Evangelista, Parma, a church in which Correggio had worked not long before, and at this stage it might have seemed that he was destined to follow in the footsteps of his senior, whose influence on his art was obvious.

But Parmigianino's brief career was much affected by the terrible events that befell Italy during its course and as early as 1521 he was forced to leave Parma, when that town was besieged by Leo X, and he took refuge in the Duchy of Milan. In 1523 he was in Rome, and it was during his stay in Rome that he did a great part of his work. When the city was sacked in 1527 he tried to escape, but was taken prisoner. Set free in the same year, he went to Bologna where in 1530 he painted the portrait of the Emperor Charles the Fifth. In 1531 he was back in Parma, painting decorations in the Church of Santa Maria della Steccata. One of his chief works of this period was a series of frescos for the Castello at Fontanellato, Count Sanvitali's domain. In 1540 he fled once more from Parma and took refuge in Casalmaggiore, where he died in the same year.

Vasari tells us that, towards the close of his life, Parmigianino became rather 'queer,' and developed propensities for alchemical research. Considering the experiences he had undergone, harried from one city to another, and, given his naturally unstable temperament, we need hardly be surprised if he took to occult studies, as a means of escape from a world that had served him so ill.

Inevitably his art was affected by the gradual change that came over his outlook on life. After starting off with a wholly sensual conception of beauty as expressed in bodies steeped in light, he moved away from reality and his art became detached, other-worldly. After falling under the spell of Correggio in his youth, he came in contact with Raphael's art during his seven years' stay in Rome. And the revelation of Raphael's magical power of transmuting all forms into beauty made an indelible impression on him. More and more he emphasized the elegance of movements, and his line became more mobile, more sinuous. Elongating necks and figures, it weaves its flowing arabesques against the light and ripples over bodies. The play of light does not abolish form but crystallizes it, giving it a strange, almost glacial aspect; indeed the figures remind us of 'Empire' statuettes, or of jewels studding the composition. Though sometimes the themes are merged in an intricate pattern of contrasted lights and shadows, the personages—especially the women—give the impression of a proud awareness of their beauty, of rejoicing in the ornaments which enhance their luster, lifting them above the everyday world. Thus Parmigianino brought something almost new to art, a subtle ambiance of luxury and gracious languor which French painters, for example those of the School of Fontainebleau, were to turn to good account.

It is indeed striking, the tendency of the men and women in Parmigianino's compositions towards a self-conscious, almost Narcissistic, idealization of their own persons. This imparts to them an air, not so much of dignity, as of quiet earnestness, pensive and aloof. The portrait of a woman in the Naples Museum illustrates to perfection this aspect of Parmigianino's art. There is good evidence to show that we have here a likeness of Antea, the painter's mistress and one of the most famous courtesans of the day. It has been observed that in this picture Parmigianino gave a new 'tone' to the portrait, by imparting to it a suggestion of the feelings he personally entertained towards the model. Here he does not over-stress the line; on the contrary he subordinates it to color-effect, while by the lavish attention given to details, he endows this woman's figure with a quality of vibrant life.

PARMIGIANINO (1503-1540). PORTRAIT OF ANTEA(?). (54½ × 34½″) PINACOTECA DEL MUSEO NAZIONALE, NAPLES.

THE VENETIAN PAINTERS

1

GIORGIONE TITIAN

POETRY AND REALITY

GIORGIONE (C. 1477-1510). THE ADORATION OF THE SHEPHERDS (DETAIL). KRESS COLLECTION, NATIONAL GALLERY
OF ART, WASHINGTON.

GIORGIONE

It was with Giorgione that Cinquecento art began in Venice; indeed he sounds the opening note of the Venetian sixteenth-century Renaissance. Though he made no drastic break with traditional art, this musician-artist changed the whole climate of Venetian painting; creating a world of wider freedom and opening horizons on a realm of art as yet uncharted.

Bellini, his senior, had enlarged the scope of mysticism in art, by extending it to renderings of nature; in Giorgione's art, nature, in all her aspects, plays the leading part.

Leonardo, his contemporary, sought to express the mystery of the universe in terms of painting; Giorgione, spontaneously identifying himself with the life of all creation, glorifies its magical beauty.

And it is to his mystical sense of 'a life in all natural things and of man's life as a part of nature' that his works owe their indefinable appeal. He opens out to us a poetic wonderland, in which art keeps her air of faintly baffling aloofness; for though, on the face of it, his work seems so forthright, it is far from being comprehensible at a first glance. And the scarcity of information about his life, together with the fact that so few of his pictures have survived, heightens our feeling of an enigma perhaps never to be solved.

His real name was Giorgio and he was born at Castelfranco. The date of his birth fell somewhere between 1475 and 1480. Vasari says, "he was thirty-four years of age when he died, in 1510, of the plague."

If his life was short, his rise to fame was rapid, and his work in great demand. Indeed Giorgione's themes became so popular that painters constantly harked back to them over a long period, and it was said that his art was responsible for the growth of a new kind of picture-fanciers and buyers: 'private collectors' as they were later to be known.

We are told of a picture Giorgione painted in 1507-1508 for the Ducal Palace, but it has disappeared. And nothing remains of the frescos he is known to have made for the Fondaco dei Tedeschi at Venice in 1508. That is all the chronological information we have about his work. There exists, however, a list of the names of his pictures, compiled by a contemporary Venetian writer, Michiel, which has much to tell us. Unfortunately only three of the pictures cited in it have survived in a condition enabling us to make a just appraisal of Giorgione's art. Around this small nucleus of certainly authentic works, art experts have grouped some other canvases presumably his; but cogent proof is wholly lacking, and many of these attributions are highly speculative, to say the least.

Yet, little as there is to go on, Giorgione's artistic personality is marked enough for us to see, and clearly to see, how great an artist he was and how vast his creative genius.

A description of his decorations at the Fondaco dei Tedeschi, given by Boschini, writing in the second half of the seventeenth century, tells us something of them. "The façade overlooking the Grand Canal was entirely covered with figures and architectural motives painted by Giorgione. Now it is almost entirely obliterated, except for some nude figures at the top, which retain traces of vivid color." Thus we gather that the work went to pieces rapidly; a very vague outline from this fresco, preserved in the Academy of Venice, gives the merest suggestion of what must have been the grandiose effect of the figures in their original condition. All the chronicles of the period concur in extolling the warmth and vigor of the color. Vasari, too, has some interesting things to say; indeed what little we know of the artist's temperament and methods comes from him. Though Vasari had but one idol, Michelangelo, paragon of painters, he shows much discrimination in his appraisal of Giorgione's art. He ranks him above all other artists "not only in Venice but everywhere," in his power of breathing life into his figures and in his handling of color, "sometimes vivid, sometimes soft, well graduated in the darker passages." But his approval is not unqualified; speaking of the Fondaco dei Tedeschi fresco, he says he (Vasari) "failed to grasp what it was all about."

GIORGIONE (C. 1477-1510). CONCERT CHAMPÊTRE. (43¼×54¼″) LOUVRE, PARIS.

This shows how little necessary Giorgione thought it to give an exact meaning to the actions of his figures. Thus, as regards the *Tempest,* the *Venus,* the *Concert* (or '*Fête*') *Champêtre* and the *Three Philosophers,* it is impossible to arrive at any really satisfactory explanation of what is being depicted. In fact these pictures demonstrate that the artist gave free rein to his creative imagination, guided only by the inner logic of his poetic vision.

Vasari tells us that "though of very humble origin, Giorgione always had perfect manners and made himself liked everywhere. He was of a loving disposition, and very fond of the lute; playing and singing so divinely that he was often invited to perform at concerts and gatherings of the best society." We seem to feel the influence of this love of music in his art. Even in his religious works such as the Castelfranco altarpiece and *The Adoration of the Shepherds,* melody of line combines with the harmony of colors to create the glamor of an old-world fairy-tale. Each figure seems to be listening to an inner music; even the trees, stones and sky tell of strange enchantments. In the *Tempest* (Venice), the absence of any normal relationship between the figures seems intensified; relinquishing their purely human functions, they are but participants in the all-pervading poetry of nature. Thus the woman and child, the soldier, the trees and houses, have become lyrical symbols, illuminated by the diffused radiance of the sky, the lights of the flesh tints, the blue-green menace of the storm. The true theme of this work, as has been rightly said, is nature. But it is not merely the 'reflection of a mood.' Giorgione's aim is not romantic self-expression; in tranquillity, he has immortalized one of those moments of poetic vision when beyond Time's horizon we glimpse eternity. Though named after the storm that broods in the offing, the picture does not strike in any sense a tragic note. The storm alarms no one; neither the spectator, nor the soldier, nor even the child in his mother's arms. Indeed the whole composition is a counterpoint of smoothly flowing light and the landscape shown by the lightning-flash breathes 'blissful ease'; we have here the happy plenitude of nature's life viewed through a poet's eye.

Indeed this canvas is not only one of Giorgione's finest works, but holds its own amongst the greatest masterpieces of all time. For never before or after Giorgione has

GIORGIONE (C. 1477-1510). THE TEMPEST. (32¼×28¾″) ACCADEMIA, VENICE.

GIORGIONE (C. 1477-1510). THE TEMPEST (DETAIL). ACCADEMIA, VENICE.

any painter conveyed his sense of the life immanent in the whole visible world with such profoundly felt emotion.

The picture known as the *Three Philosophers* (in the Vienna Museum) shows three male figures, clothed in different ways, in a glade. Through a gap in the trees we glimpse a town in the distance. In the foreground a hooded ancient stands beside a man in oriental attire, while a young man seated a little way off is gazing into the middle distance, lost in a daydream. Here, too, we are at a loss to say just what this picture has to tell.

Recently it has been suggested that the figures portray Aristotle (the old man) and Averroes (the man in oriental costume), while the young man lost in contemplation is a personification of the new philosophy of nature.

Far-fetched as this explanation may seem, it is in keeping with the ambiance of the world in which Giorgione moved. Not only was there a keen interest in knowledge of all kinds, and not only were the Venetians of the day justly proud of the high cultural level their city had attained, but this culture had permeated their very lives. And what Giorgione expresses here is the complete fusion of the thinking mind with the life of nature. With soft, warm tones, and with the drawing minimized in order to exalt the luminosity of the colors, the artist's soaring imagination has created an all-pervasive harmony between the figures and the landscape.

GIORGIONE (C. 1477-1510). CONCERT CHAMPÊTRE (DETAIL). LOUVRE, PARIS.

In the *Concert Champêtre* the theme is frankly musical, and rarely has an artist orchestrated so melodiously the song of nature. Everything seems to be listening to it in an enchanted silence; the landscape, the nude woman at the well no less than the two players whose gaze is a silent echo of their music, and even the trees, the earth itself, seem spell-bound. Here we have a fusion of all Giorgione's themes. And if the attribution of this work to him has been disputed, it is because the proportions are bolder, the drawing broader than is usual in his work. The fullness of the forms he gives his figures bears out an observation made by the writer Zanetti, in a work that was published in 1771. Speaking of Giorgione, Zanetti discusses the polemics which in the Cinquecento split up the admirers of Michelangelo and the defenders of the new Venetian art into opposing camps, the bone of contention being the question whether sculpture should be given the primacy in art, as against painting. With this in mind, Paolo Pino had drawn attention to a work by Giorgione which by a play of lights and mirrors fully rendered a whole body 'in the round.' And Zanetti paid homage to Giorgione for having succeeded in giving painting "its true character of art." "The forcefulness and roundness of his figures," Zanetti continues, "do not prevent him, as they prevent other painters, from giving the flesh color its ardent, almost ruddy beauty, as though gleams of fire were playing on the skin."

We find the same poetic transfiguration in the *Sleeping Venus* (Dresden). The sensuous appeal of this nude body is enhanced by the white drapery on which it lies, while its smoothly flowing lines are paralleled in those of a landscape bathed in evening light. Thus the hill seems almost to uphold the sleeping head; the landscape opening out in the background is a visual echo of the body's repose. The shimmering air imparts a vibrant life to the gleams that hover on the body, the trees, the red of the drapery and the closed eyelids of the sleeping woman. Sensuality is here no doubt, but something more; the painter wishes, it seems, to convey a blind, unconditional surrender of the conscious being to the eternal, never-changing life of mother earth.

GIORGIONE (C. 1477-1510). THE SLEEPING VENUS. (43 × 68 ¾") GEMÄLDEGALERIE, DRESDEN.
The original being inaccessible, this plate has been engraved after the replica of Mr Franz Hanfstaengl, at Munich.

GIORGIONE (C. 1477-1510). THE TEMPEST (DETAIL). ACCADEMIA, VENICE.

Giorgione's art is one of the loftiest expressions of the culture, at once refined and addicted to sensual pleasure, of Venice of the Cinquecento. He loved the light of Venice, her sudden glints of color, that haze of broken lights, the beauty of a dream, enveloping stones and trees, earth and sky. But, with his love for all God's works, Giorgione lifted the Venetian dream on to a higher plane. Sublimated in the ecstasy of his poetic vision of the world, his natural responses became an act of faith, and every picture from his brush voices a hymn of praise to all creation.

P.I. 2 — 63

—   —

GIORGIONE (C. 1477-1510)-TITIAN (1477/87-1576). MUSICIAN, THE CONCERT (DETAIL). PITTI PALACE, FLORENCE.

TITIAN (1477/87-1576). VENUS AND CUPID (DETAIL). UFFIZI, FLORENCE.

TITIAN

When we compare the lives of Titian and Giorgione, who otherwise had so much in common, we cannot but be struck by the marked contrast between their respective careers. Giorgione, the poet-artist, died young like the hero of a romantic tale—in his early thirties—, was almost from the start in full possession of his powers, and the world his genius created has the enchantment of joyous youth.

Whereas that Herculean artist Titian, the 'Grand Old Man' of Italian art, progressed from strength to strength throughout a life that almost touched its hundredth year, and the 'constant' of his art is its robust maturity.

The date of his birth is uncertain; most probably 1477, though some date it much later, 1486 or 1487. Born in the village of Pieve di Cadore, he came at a very early age to Venice, and studied first under Gentile, then under Giovanni Bellini. In 1508 he worked with Giorgione on the frescos at the Fondaco dei Tedeschi, painting the side facing the town, while Giorgione painted that beside the Grand Canal. None of these frescos has survived. In 1511 he was at Padua painting for the Scuola del Santo and the Scuola del Carmine frescos which, while primarily descriptive, are enlivened by strong contrasts of light and shade.

On his return to Venice Titian embarked on a large-scale composition in the Hall of Great Council of the Ducal Palace, a task on which he set much store, being well aware that it would establish him securely amongst the leading painters of the time—which explains why he declined a proposal he should go to Rome. In 1516 he succeeded Giovanni Bellini as official painter to La Serenissima, and subsequently he contracted to paint the portraits of each Doge when he took up his post. Though in the 1577 fire Titian's decorations in the Hall of Great Council were destroyed, this early period was an exceedingly prolific one and we can follow his artistic development in the many pictures that have come down to us.

Giorgione's boldness in his handling of certain themes had impressed the connoisseurs of the day and indeed wrought changes in the general outlook on art, and while still under his influence Titian kept to these themes, over a considerable period. Old records tell us that he was instructed to complete the canvases Giorgione had left unfinished at his death; indeed the spirit animating the two artists was so similar that in some pictures it is impossible precisely to distinguish the share of each. *The Concert* (Pitti, Florence) was for a long while attributed to Giorgione, perhaps because of the intense spirituality of the face of the monk in the foreground; though actually the dramatic power of this same figure is eminently characteristic of Titian's genius.

Many of Titian's non-religious compositions have points in common with those of Giorgione: for instance, nude figures of women that seem to melt into the landscape, nature treated as a creative force, broken gleams of color, and—most notably of all—the insertion of 'motives' that have no bearing on the main theme and indeed no logical justification for their presence. Thus in the famous *Sacred and Profane Love* we see two women seated on either side of a well, with a landscape background. Actually, it is not known what this picture was intended to convey; its present name was given it long after the painter's death. He is said to have called it *The Bath*—a vague name, explaining nothing.

At first sight there would seem to be no difference between the pictorial qualities and conceptions of Titian in this early phase, and Giorgione's. Still already we can detect in the former's work a greater simplification of details and a livelier sensibility in the passage-work and tonal contrasts—the result of a craftsmanship superior to Giorgione's, but lacking his poetic charm.

Inaugurated by Giorgione, this kind of painting had become so popular that Titian's work was greatly in demand. When, summoned by Alfonso d'Este, he made a stay at the Ferrara Court (1516), he was given orders for three pictures on mythological subjects: the *Venus Worship* (ca. 1518), the *Bacchanalia* (ca. 1520), whose theme, taken from Ariosto, was suggested to the painter by the Duke, and *Bacchus and Ariadne*, completed later, in 1523.

In all these works, especially in the two first, the fluent play of light on bodies, highlights on the skin, and the sunlight rippling over the sky and across the trees create a ceaseless undulation, like the rhythm of a dance. And all these gleaming bodies and glowing colors convey a festal mood, a careless rapture, the painter's frank delight in radiant sunshine, women's beauty and the mere fact of living.

Whereas Giorgione expressed his innate pantheism in a poetic vision of nature, Titian, more sensual in his responses, yields whole-heartedly to the pleasure of bathing trees and bodies in a glow of lambent light, a reflex of the joy he takes in them.

As the years went on Titian aimed at ever more striking effects of movement in terms of light and shade. In his famous *Assunta*, made for the church of Santa Maria dei Frari and exhibited in 1518, he has completely freed himself from Giorgione's influence. The religious nature of this subject called for a very different treatment; it was the might of religion, the Church's great mission of enlightenment, that he was seeking to convey. Thus the *Assunta*, one of a long series of great altarpieces, reveals the desire of the artist to find a perfect art form for the officially established religion of his day. With the concentrated violence of the movements of light and shade, he achieved his lofty purpose; in pursuance of a nobly balanced lay-out, the shadows bathe in subtly graduated tones the human figures, while the sky, a blaze of ever-growing light, seems to be drawing up towards it the Madonna. Here, it must be admitted, there is something slightly rhetorical in the attitudes—it is as though the effort to reconcile religious idealism with this forceful presentation had proved almost too much for the painter. But we find nothing of this sort in the altarpiece for the church of San Domenico at Ancona. That bare tree in the background imparts to the whole landscape a soaring movement, an echo, as it were, of the figure of the Saint, telling out majestically

TITIAN (1477/87-1576). SACRED AND PROFANE LOVE. LANDSCAPE (DETAIL). GALLERIA BORGHESE, ROME.

against the brightness of the drifting clouds. And in the altarpiece which he completed in 1526, for the noble House of Pesaro, Titian sublimated his love of all things human into a superb vision of the noble and transcendent. The lay-out is diagonal, its focal highlight being the Madonna, and the two big pillars giving the scene its balance and enclosing the figures in a structure which, for all its massiveness, lies open to the sky, participate in the action with their moving play of shadows, while imparting to the painting as a whole the solidity of marble.

Titian's obvious desire to keep a firm grip on reality—his own life bears this out—inevitably drew him towards portraiture. And the tradition of the portrait bulked large in Venetian art. The notabilities of Venice, as well as many persons of high rank in Italy and abroad, found in Titian just the portraitist they needed to perpetuate their fame. After the Este court, that of Mantua called in the painter. There was keen competition between this new patron and Alfonso d'Este for the services of Titian and he was a frequent visitor at both courts. When Federico Gonzaga decided to acquire a series of pictures of the twelve Caesars for his residence at Mantua his choice fell on Titian, who meanwhile was busily employed painting the leading figures of the various courts of Italy. Records dated 1527 tell of his sending Federico Gonzaga a portrait of Aretino—which indicates that the long friendship between the painter and this man of letters, the "founder of modern journalism' as Mr. Berenson describes him, had already begun. Though his reputation was of the worst and he had been banished from Rome, Aretino "was in touch with the most eminent personalities of the day." Thus he could write, with that mixture of humor and vanity so characteristic of him, that the staircase of his home was "as much worn by their steps as the paving-stones of the Capitol by the wheels of the triumphal cars." Titian's association with this brilliant adventurer served him well, for Aretino sang his praises everywhere. Also Aretino's letters tell us many interesting facts about the painter's career. No doubt there was a practical motive, of a financial order, behind Aretino's vast enthusiasm for his friend's art, but it is also clear that Titian and he had temperamentally much in common. In a famous letter written to the painter during an absence from Venice Aretino gives a vivid description of the lagoon, the colors of the sky and water, which might well be that of one of Titian's pictures. And it shows us that this Tuscan was so taken with the atmosphere of Venice that he had come to appreciate only the pictures painted by Venetian artists.

His knack of 'registering' a face at that crucial psychological moment when the man's true nature reveals itself, while adding a touch of nobility to it, accounts for the popularity of Titian's portraits with contemporaries, and especially with members of the Italian courts. Even in pictures with religious themes such as the *Presentation of the Virgin*, the composition is so arranged as to bring out individual characteristics in the groups; that famous figure of the old woman at the foot of the staircase has the vividness of a portrait done from the life. More and more Titian tended to aim at keying up the presentation of his subject to a technical proficiency hitherto undreamt of. Indeed in the *Portrait of Francis I* at the Louvre, the model for which was some French painting, and no less when he paints his daughter Lavinia in all her youthful grace, the consummate craftsmanship almost seems to hamper the free rendering of the subject. Elsewhere the play of light and shade in the colors and the atmosphere create the real 'climate' of the portraits, as in the case of the so-called *Young Englishman* (in the Pitti, Florence), which was actually the portrait of Riminaldi, secretary to the Duke of Ferrara. The dark mass of the body emerges from the neutral hues of the background, deliberately blurred, one would say, so as to bring out

TITIAN (1477/87-1576). NUDES. (11 × 17″) CHARCOAL. UFFIZI, FLORENCE.

TITIAN (1477/87-1576). BACCHANALIA. (68½×75½") PRADO, MADRID.

more strongly the light vibrating in the face and hands. The white patch of the collarette, framing the neck, emphasizes the face rising above it, and a sudden flash of light kindling the pupils gives an almost hypnotic intensity to the gaze.

While in such a portrait as this, Titian transmutes his direct experience of reality into something far nobler, hardly of this life, there are times when his subjects prompt him to keeping nearer to reality and portraying the world under its more ordinary aspects. When, round about 1532, he first came in touch with the Urbino Court (which he continued visiting for some forty years) he made several portraits of its leading members. But he also painted the *Venus in an Interior* now in the Uffizi. Here the artist frankly transforms the mythological subject into a scene of everyday life. The beauty of the woman's body is brought out to the full by the light enveloping it, exalting it, flooding it with life, and, to strengthen its immediate appeal, the painter has placed the goddess in a typical Venetian great lady's room, with two maids in attendance. Between Giorgione's harmonious fusion of the dream and real life and Titian's boldly passionate response to woman's beauty, much ground has been covered.

Titian was more sought after than ever; the rulers of the Italian courts plied him with invitations and when, in 1545, he went to Rome he was welcomed with open arms not

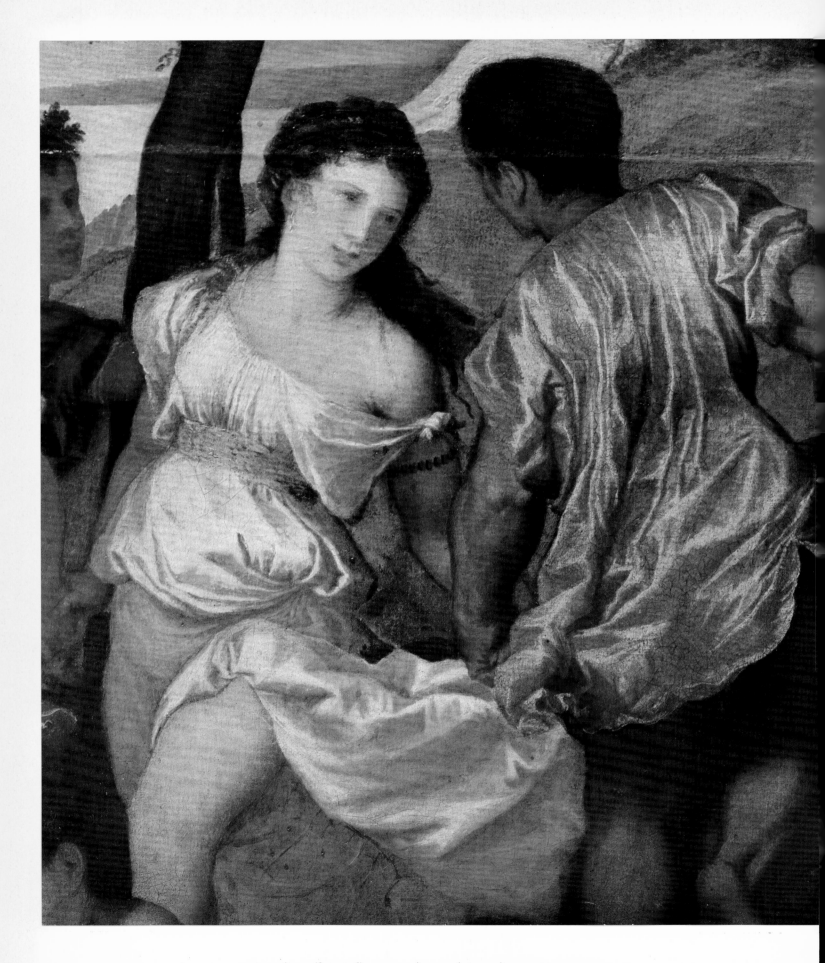

TITIAN (1477/87-1576). BACCHANALIA (DETAIL). PRADO, MADRID.

TITIAN (1477/87-1576). BACCHANALIA (DETAIL). PRADO, MADRID.

TITIAN (1477/87-1576). SO-CALLED PORTRAIT OF RIMINALDI (DETAIL). PITTI PALACE, FLORENCE.

only by Cardinal Bembo but by the Pope himself. In a letter to Aretino he tells of his enthusiastic reception, and in the following year he was nominated 'citizen of Rome' with due pomp and ceremony. It was now that he had an opportunity of seeing Raphael's and Michelangelo's work in the Sistine. But, though fully conscious of the compelling power of Michelangelo and his majestic treatment of volumes, the effect of this experience on his art was fleeting. Indeed it is in the portrait he then made of Pope Paul III and his nephews that his unique personality makes its presence felt most clearly. Forms are varied by the all-pervading ebb and flow of light, which gives a vast range of gradations to the dominant red, and in this symphony of ever-changing, smoothly flowing tones, some rippling brush-strokes on the old Pope's face suggest its contrast with the younger faces. Thus the advanced age of the Pope is indicated, not by representational devices, but by purely pictorial methods.

Great as was his popularity with the highest circles of Italy, it was in the court of the Emperor Charles V that Titian's renown touched high-water mark. At the suggestion of the Duke of Mantua he was invited to paint the Emperor's portrait on the occasion of his coronation at Bologna. Three years later he was given the rank of Count Palatine, a distinction carrying with it a number of privileges as well as setting an official seal on the high esteem he already enjoyed. The letters patent describe in glowing terms his lofty merits as a painter and his power of rendering his sitters' faces 'to the life.'

When at a very early age Titian came from his mountain home to Venice, that city was at the height of its political power. And, in other cities too, the aristocracy was becoming alive to its high responsibilities. One of the secrets of Titian's success lies partly in the happy

TITIAN (1477/87-1576). VENUS AND CUPID (DETAIL). UFFIZI, FLORENCE.

TITIAN (1477/87-1576). ST FRANCIS (DETAIL FROM THE VIRGIN AND CHILD, ST FRANCIS, ST ALVISE AND THE DONOR).
FROM THE CHURCH OF S. DOMENICO, MUSEO CIVICO, ANCONA.

skill with which, coming as he did of a stock of hardy peasants, he adjusted himself to the aristocratic climate of the age. Truth to tell, his appreciation of all that was elegant and distinguished was innate, and the Emperor's court at once gratified and stimulated this instinct. In the aristocratic ambiance of sixteenth-century Spain he found, to perfection, what he had always dreamed of; here was a world built to an heroic measure and conscious of its nobility, and here were men who expressed this in the proud aloofness of their bearing, their cult of pomp and circumstance.

When, in 1548, the painter went to meet the Emperor at Augsburg he made portraits of all the members of the court, notably that of the victor of Muhlberg in his ornate, ceremonial attire. In this canvas (now at the Prado) the storm-clouds slashed with red, the black horse plumed and caparisoned in gold and silver, the concentrated tension of the rider's attitude and the movement of the horse—all conspire to lift this painting to an epic level, and make the Emperor an effigy "of Destiny itself approaching, silent and unavoidable."

In 1550, at the convention of the Diet, Titian again went to Augsburg, where amongst other portraits he made one of the Infante (Philip). After his return to Venice Titian continued sending pictures, dealing with 'profane' as well as religious subjects, to the Emperor and subsequently to Philip II, who had ascended the throne of Spain.

Thus Titian was loaded with all the honors that the great ones of the earth could confer on him; his renown had traversed the frontiers of Europe, and, even though the

TITIAN (1477/87-1576). OLD WOMAN SELLING CHICKENS. PRESENTATION OF THE VIRGIN (DETAIL).
ACCADEMIA, VENICE.

TITIAN (1477/87-1576). CHARLES V AT THE BATTLE OF MUHLBERG. (130 × 109½″) PRADO, MADRID.

authorities commissioning his work were often remiss in paying for it, his business acumen had enabled him to amass a considerable fortune. Now that he was back in Venice, he decided he had had enough of travelling—if people wanted to see him, let them come to Venice—and, except for a brief stay at Brescia, never again quitted his adoptive city. Knowing that his work would be unquestioningly accepted by his patrons, he devoted himself entirely to his art, and to this period belong the pictures in which he expresses himself most spontaneously, most freely, and gives the fullest scope to his amazing creative energy.

The dramatic effect of those touches of color—almost, we might say, flung upon the canvas—from which emerges, treated on purely pictorial, not realistic, lines, the body of the saint in the Leningrad *St Sebastian*, marks a peak point in Titian's art.

In the *Adam and Eve* (in the Prado) he gave another illustration of the possibilities of constructive color, which here conveys the strength of the man's body as contrasted with the luminous mass of the woman's.

TITIAN (1477/87-1576). PORTRAIT OF PAUL III WITH HIS NEPHEWS ALESSANDRO AND OTTAVIO FARNESE. (78½ × 68½") PINACOTECA DEL MUSEO NAZIONALE, NAPLES.

During this last period of activity Titian painted several more pictures on non-religious themes. Some of these, painted at successive stages of his career, suffice taken by themselves to enable us to follow the evolution of his art. Thus we see how, from the *Bacchanalia* of his youth to such works as the *Shepherd and Nymph* (Vienna) and the *Danaë* (Prado, Madrid), his technique gradually changed, adding a note of spirituality to his vision—a poetic transmutation worked by the alchemy of light and color. Woelfflin described the *Venus* of the Uffizi (dated ca. 1537) as "an image radiating brightness and natural life, within a seeming nonchalance." There is indeed something of magic here, yet here, too, we have indications of the very special realism that was Titian's. Conspicuous in his last phase was the vibrancy of his brushwork, but the dramatic tension of his religious scenes was gone.

Finally, we have a portrait of himself in extreme old age. The figure seems hardly more than a glimmering wraith; the body is a dark blur, a weak light illuminates the hand, and the face, poised between light and shadow, belongs no longer to the real world but solely to the world of painting. When, in 1566, Vasari visited the aged artist, he was conscious that here was painting raised to its purest, most transcendent 'power,' yet somehow its full meaning eluded him. It is interesting to find him saying that if one looks closely at a work by Titian, one can make nothing out; to make its effect, it has to be seen from a distance. Vasari could not be expected to guess that in this respect Titian's art was pointing the way to an art that was to arise several centuries later, beginning with Impressionism. Throughout his very long career (he died in 1576) the genius of Titian owed its compelling power to the warmth and directness of his response to life, and to his firm belief in the value of painting in itself. "The ideal that life can be enriched through art," writes Dvorak, "took its rise with Titian." And that no doubt is why the art of this great sixteenth-century painter made so strong a mark on the following generations, and still seems so prodigiously alive.

TITIAN (1477/87-1576). DANAË. (50×70") PRADO, MADRID.

TITIAN (1477/87-1576). ADAM AND EVE. (94×73″) PRADO, MADRID.

TITIAN (1477/87-1576). SELF-PORTRAIT. (33½×25½″) PRADO, MADRID.

2

SEBASTIANO DEL PIOMBO
LOTTO - SAVOLDO
BASSANO - MORONI

SEBASTIANO DEL PIOMBO

At first sight it may seem strange that a painter can have drawn his inspiration from three such different worlds as those of Giorgione, Raphael and Michelangelo, and yet retain a distinct, coherent personality of his own. Moreover, Sebastiano del Piombo who brought off this unusual feat is not to be described merely as an eclectic. He may have lacked the driving force of personal genius and thus failed to discover any strongly original theme, but once a theme was given, his talent was such that he transformed it, made it his.

Sebastiano del Piombo (the family name was Luciani) was born about 1485 at Venice and began by studying under Giovanni Bellini; but, attracted by the 'modern manner' and its 'blaze of color' he took to working with Giorgione. We are told by the Italian humanist Michiel that the latter's *The Three Philosophers* was completed by Sebastiano; this shows how close was the contact between the two artists. It is clear that in the artistic circle frequented by Sebastiano, Giorgione's personality reigned supreme, and it is also interesting to learn from records of the time that, like Giorgione, Sebastiano del Piombo was a musician as well as a painter. "An excellent performer on the lute," Pino writes, and Vasari says that he, too, made portraits of musicians. These remarks confirm the close relations between the artist and the cultured *élite* of Venice. Moreover in the few extant works of this period of his youth we can see how enthusiastically Sebastiano adopted the methods of Giorgione as regards brushwork and the rendering of light. His forms, however, are conceived more broadly and their harmony is simpler. Probably the young artist had been impressed by the frescos of the Fondaco dei Tedeschi, where we are told that "figures of large proportions were displayed in pillared vistas."

Anyhow it is clear that what Sebastiano aimed at, from the start, was effects of masses rendered with the maximum of movement. True, the group of three women in the altarpiece of the Church of S. Giovanni Crisostomo was still so much like the work of Giorgione that Vasari attributes it to him. But once Sebastiano left Venice he entered a realm of art whose spiritual climate was different indeed from that of Giorgione's, and in which movement, agitation, even violence were everything.

In 1511 Sebastiano went to Rome on the invitation of the banker Agostino Chigi, whose villa (La Farnesina) he decorated along with Raphael and under his supervision. Not only did he strike up a close friendship with Raphael, but he took over from him his repertory of forms, lock, stock and barrel. Nevertheless, the discrepancy between Roman and Venetian art was too great for him to be able, without an effort, to strike a balance between two so different art-worlds.

On the other hand that famous portrait of *La Fornarina* (in the Uffizi), dated 1512, is remarkable for the exquisite purity of its line, though in its color and the richness of its tones we find reminiscences of Giorgione. With the result that, here, ideal vision and the emotional appeal of the woman's body are most happily combined. Over a long period this work was attributed to Raphael; a natural enough mistake when we remember how great was Raphael's influence on the Venetian, who, in any case benefited not a little thereby. It encouraged him to simplify his forms, and "imparted a new balance to the rhythm and lay-out of Sebastiano's means of expression, after that violent, indeed aggressive phase of the Farnesina frescos." Though Sebastiano del Piombo was so strongly influenced by his contacts with Raphael, the latter, likewise, was influenced by the sudden revelation of Venetian color. But Sebastiano's personality was not compelling enough to impart more than an accent, distinctive though it was, to Roman painting. It was in the same year, 1512, that Michelangelo's work on the Sistine ceiling was revealed to the public, and while it made a deep though not decisive impression on Raphael, it marked the turning point in the art of the Venetian; he plunged forthwith into the superhuman, monumental world of Michelangelo. The decorations he made for the Church of S. Pietro in Montorio (begun in 1516 and finished only in 1524) show the great stress he now laid on broadly constructed masses and on the

SEBASTIANO DEL PIOMBO (C. 1485-1547). PIETA. (106×88½″) MUSEO CIVICO, VITERBO.

movement of bodies, though transitions of tones and shadings-off of color are not ruled out. In 1517 he painted his *Resurrection of Lazarus*, vying with Raphael's *Transfiguration*, and his letters of the period have much to say of the hostility that had arisen between the school of Raphael and the disciples of Michelangelo. They also show how completely the Venetian was dominated by the personality of the painter of the Sistine; he looked to him for guidance almost obsequiously, not only asking him for suggestions and advice, but begging him to sketch out models for his paintings. Though he had been so friendly with Raphael Sebastiano del Piombo joined the camp of Michelangelo's admirers with surprising promptness. The records tell of his great affection for Michelangelo and, speaking of his art, somewhat overstress his "Michelangelism." True, Sebastiano availed himself of Michelangelo's drawings; but we must not forget that he was naturally inclined towards a plastic treatment of forms, and that indications of this could be seen even in his quite early works (as noted also by Vasari).

The *Pietà* he painted for the Church of S. Vincenzo at Viterbo marks a culminating point of his art. The bodies are transfigured by the color; the landscape background, built up of highly skillful transitions from grey to brown, implements the tragic effect of the scene. Here there are still echoes of Giorgione, especially in the harmonious blending of nature and the human figures. The sheen of moonlight playing across the landscape seems like an accompaniment to the grief rending the Mother's heart as she contemplates her dead Son stretched at her feet. Starting from the palely gleaming body of Christ, the emotional tension rises to its climax in the face of the Madonna; then dies away into the darkness of the background faintly lit by the rising moon. Rarely has a painter succeeded in achieving a composition so monumental in effect by the use of emphatic, skillfully correlated colors.

Though Sebastiano del Piombo never again achieved so compellingly the transmutation of color and volumes, some of his later works bear unmistakably the stamp of his personality, even where we know Michelangelo to have supplied preliminary sketches and given a start to the drawing. But the friendship between the two artists after lasting many years came to an abrupt end in 1533, perhaps because of Sebastiano's ill-advised persistence in wanting Michelangelo to paint his *Last Judgement* in oils, a medium which he disdained. "Oil painting is an art for women," he once remarked.

In his last phase, Sebastiano del Piombo treated Michelangelo's world on schematic, strictly formal lines, eliminating its natural content, and thus tending toward Mannerist procedure. His output, too, was small during these last years of his life, which ended in 1547. Vasari says that he had made too much money, had no need to work, and, whether out of fatigue or laziness, had almost given up painting. Also perhaps a phase of depression he was passing through at the time contributed to this. In 1531, after the sack of Rome, he wrote in a letter, "I no longer feel myself the same Bastiano as in the past." And, elsewhere, he says: "Now I have enough to live on, I don't want to work any more; there are men today who can do in two months what took me two years to do, and I suspect that, if I go on living long enough, I shall see the day when nothing more is left to paint."

Vasari also says that he could have been "the king of painters, but failed because of his carelessness," while Aretino described his art as nothing short of "miraculous." Though modern authorities are disposed to rank him amongst the great artists of his time, he comes in for not a little criticism. In sum, we may say that he was a powerfully gifted painter, and to his brush are due some of the most outstanding works of his century.

LOTTO

Lorenzo Lotto was born about 1480, in Venice, and his career spanned the first half of the sixteenth century. Thus he belonged to the generation which saw the rise of Giorgione's 'new manner,' and witnessed the triumphal progress of Titian's prolific genius. Lotto's place, however, was outside the main stream of the new Venetian art; he had not the carefree temperament of his great contemporaries, and turned to other masters for his inspiration.

LORENZO LOTTO (C. 1480-1556). ST JEROME IN THE WILDERNESS.
FRAGMENT. LOUVRE, PARIS.

LORENZO LOTTO (C. 1480-1556). PORTRAIT OF AN UNKNOWN MAN (DETAIL). BRERA, MILAN.

In the Louvre *St Jerome*, a work of his youth dated 1506, influences of the school of Giovanni Bellini can still be traced. But the delicate sensibility with which he treats this landscape is quite unlike the joyous pantheism of Giorgione, whose approach to art was, nevertheless, like his, by way of Bellini. In this picture the human figure plays the part of a patch of color, the pink garment catches the wavering gleams filtering through the leafy trees, and is recalled in the sheen of a sky dappled with drifting clouds. This work is imbued with deep poetic feeling, the painter's direct response to the woodland's green tranquillity. And in other pictures by him we often seem to feel the presence of this direct inspiration.

At an early stage, before he left Venice, Lotto was much impressed by Dürer's art, with its suggestions of a more vigorous handling of line. In 1509, after staying in several towns of Central Italy, he came to Rome, summoned by Pope Julius II who commissioned him to paint, along with other artists, the Stanze of the Vatican. But when Raphael arrived, he had to make over the work to him, and the paintings he had begun were destroyed.

LORENZO LOTTO (C. 1480-1556). PORTRAIT OF AN UNKNOWN MAN (DETAIL). BRERA, MILAN.

However, he stayed on in Rome until 1512 and thus could see a large part of the work done by Raphael. This encouraged him towards a more emphatic modeling of bodies and a new conception of the relations between forms and color. Lotto's Roman sojourn was not time lost, for here he learned to combine the tendencies of Venetian painting with those of Rome.

From 1513 on, he lived for nearly ten years at Bergamo, and much of his work is to be seen there. He also travelled in the Italian Marches and Venetia, staying several times at Venice. He was much appreciated by the public of the provinces, and this was a factor in the shaping of his style; thus, so far, he was untouched by Titian's art, then predominant at Venice. This secluded life, far from any of the great art centers, led the artist, already sensitive and shy by nature, to withdraw still more into himself. During this period we find a strain of fantasy, sometimes bizarre but always full of curious charm, entering into his work. But also we cannot help feeling a lack of real homogeneity in his vision of the world. Towards the close of his life he made his retreat in Loreto where he painted some pictures for the Palazzo Apostolico, and where he died, in 1556.

It was in this last phase that he underwent Titian's influence, moving towards a more sumptuous art and subordinating plastic form to effects of light and shade. Lotto was an earnest, simple, good-hearted man, "kindness itself," as Titian said of him. And it was this innate humility which kept him from the grandiose, the monumental, and led him to concentrate on the figure, treating it with a freedom as to plastic form exceeding even that of Titian. Thus his *Portrait of an Unknown Man* (Brera, Milan) has a sensitivity admirably rendered and vibrant with life. He uses breaks in the line rather than touches of color for indicating the structure of the figure, thus calling forth, across the shifting lights of the chiaroscuro, the living presence of the model. We may picture Lotto as a man of the highest principles, of sensitive perceptions and a gift for spontaneous expression. Still he lacked that tenacity of purpose which an artist needs if he is to make steady progress towards a truly personal style, and thus he cannot rank amongst the greatest painters of the Venetian school of the Cinquecento. Nevertheless his personality is one of the most attractive, and perhaps the most poignantly emotive, of the age.

SAVOLDO

While Lotto's art stands apart from the new trends set in motion by the first generation of the sixteenth century, that of Savoldo (born about 1480) falls obviously into line with the new Venetian painting of the Cinquecento. True, his pictures owe much to Giorgione, to whom they constantly hark back. But under the forcible stamp of Savoldo's personality their meaning is completely changed. Vasari described his work as "wayward and sophisticated," and it must be admitted that the composition of his pictures sometimes borders on the theatrical, owing to the violent contrasts of light and shade, and attitudes that seem less lifelike than contrived. In spite of this, his art has a highly personal accent of its own. Sometimes in his religious scenes he gives us quiet, intimate glimpses of the countryside and daily life. And with his particular fondness for the ordinary things and objects he saw around him and in nature, Savoldo inclines towards some of those homely themes we find in Flemish painting.

True, Savoldo transposes Titian's soaring vision to a more ordinary level, on which the aristocracy is replaced by well-to-do countryfolk. Yet his fervent religious faith works wonders with the modest scenes and details of everyday life. Without repudiating their lot as tillers of the soil, Savoldo's peasants idealize it, and his religious pictures, such as *The Adoration of the Shepherds*, have an intimate charm all their own. The sudden gleams of light, his careful renderings of the textures of wood, stone and garments, and his accuracy in descriptive detail, impart a touch of nobility even to the humblest scenes he paints.

Born, it would seem, at Brescia, Savoldo was trained in Venice. In 1508 he enrolled in the Painter's Guild at Florence and Leonardo's influence is perceptible in all his subsequent work. It is not known if he halted at Milan when he was on his way to Verona, where he had been commissioned to paint an altarpiece. But whatever elements Savoldo took over from Lombard painting he handled in a wholly personal way; he aimed at rendering reality objectively—that is to say, as if perceived from without and not re-created by the painter's imagination. This attitude, characteristic also of such painters as Boltraffio, pointed the way to the Still Life.

Despite his travels, Savoldo spent most of his life in Venice. In 1548 Aretino spoke of him as "very old", and from this time on we hear no more of him.

Throughout his career Savoldo showed an ever greater assiduity in stressing the play of light on color, and achieved highly realistic light effects by playing them off against blocks of darkness. And in *Tobias and the Angel* (Borghese, Rome) he imparts to the angel an ethereal whiteness, making us feel this is a visitant from another world. Though as compared with Leonardo's angels Savoldo's have a certain heaviness, he resembles him in the aura of otherworldly purity which he gives their figures. Here the rhythm started by the angel's profile is carried on into the arabesque of the outstretched wings—to such effect that in this picture Venetian color seems to impart new splendor to Leonardo's lofty vision.

Elsewhere, in a picture at the Metropolitan Museum, the luminosity of the drapery is carried to a grandiose intensity, thanks to a lay-out wholly in terms of contrasted light and dark. In his portraits, instead of trying to bring out the individual personality, he looks at the sitter from the outside and treats him rather as a social type. The model is shown well in the foreground and close up, thus occupying a large part of the canvas. Thus the part played by the landscape is no more than that of a very distant accompaniment to the figure, which has, so to speak, the solo part. Elsewhere he depicts a fluteplayer in a room, with his instrument to his lips: here the light and muted colors are delightfully appropriate, skillfully adjusted to 'the condition of music.'

We have few works by Savoldo, yet they suffice to prove that, in this dazzling phase of Venetian art, artists of the day could handle minor themes without lessening the vigor and effectiveness of their creative inspiration.

BASSANO

An afterglow as it were of the great Venetian art of the Cinquecento often transforms the compositions of even the most provincial, least ambitious painters of the small outlying townships into something rich and strange, an iridescent maze of colors spangled with jewel-like gleams of light. And Jacopo Bassano—his real name was Da Ponte—who was born between 1510 and 1515 would probably have been no more than a relatively undistinguished illustrator of the stock themes of contemporary art, had his visual imagination not been fired by the work of the great Venetians.

Tintoretto drenches his colors in light effects, and Veronese lightens his darker passages so as to make good a color-scheme in which he wishes bright hues to predominate. Bassano handles his colors much on the lines of Tintoretto but imparts to them a vivacity and intensity that makes them sparkle even more than Tintoretto's. Emerging from deep shadows, they acquire a luminosity almost magical in its effect—flakes of living light shot through with vivid color. Indeed this use of color-light is the secret of Bassano's art, the real theme of his pictures; for the actual subject depicted is, to his mind, of quite secondary importance.

He was born at Bassano, a market-town near Vicenza in the heart of the Venetian province, and came of a well-to-do, typically rural family. Though he made several visits to Venice, he always lived in his hometown, where he enjoyed the high esteem of all around him. In 1541, and again subsequently, he was exempted from paying any taxes "in view of the excellence of his painting." In 1549 he was offered the post of town councillor, but

GIOVANNI GIROLAMO SAVOLDO (C. 1480-AFTER 1548). TOBIAS AND THE ANGEL (DETAIL). GALLERIA BORGHESE, ROME.

declined it. He died in 1592 and his sons, whose sense of filial respect excelled their originality, reiterated on their canvases their father's themes. This brief account of the painter's life may serve to throw some light on certain characteristics of Bassano's work.

During the first stage of his career, his art kept more or less in step with that which lesser painters were practising in the shadow of the great Venetian masters. Though there is no record that Bassano ever worked in Titian's 'school,' it is clear that he was greatly drawn towards that master's art. But, at the same time, he was influenced by some of the procedures of Roman Mannerism. While there is no certain proof that he ever made the traditional journey to Rome, an seventeenth-century writer says that "having seen the 'court' of Raphael and Michelangelo, Bassano applied himself to the study of the muscles of the body and became the most competent, in this branch, of its Venetian exponents." Which amounts to saying that, in his art at this stage, the painter took up a position analogous to that of certain Mannerists.

It was only relatively late in life that Bassano—in his religious compositions—came distinctively into his own. Though Savoldo, amongst others, had a way of including in his representations of sacred subjects elements of ordinary daily life, he always remained, so to say, 'objective' as regards the scene portrayed. Bassano, however, had no qualms about transplanting his religious compositions into the atmosphere of the countryside he knew so well. We are shown typical haylofts and farmyard animals, while the men and women, frankly Italian peasants, go about their ordinary occupations. But Bassano is essentially a colorist. Under his brush what might be a commonplace *genre* scene, without any special interest, becomes a vast field of lambent light, in which the colors under the highlights gleam like jewels. Thus provincial though he is, and lacking real culture, Bassano, by dint of his creative inspiration, makes of these familiar religious scenes wonderlands of sensuous beauty. Hence the vast renown of his art not only in Venice but beyond the frontiers of Italy.

JACOPO BASSANO (1510/15-1592). THE ADORATION OF THE SHEPHERDS. (30×37″) GALLERIA BORGHESE, ROME.

MORONI

Giovanni Battista Moroni, the date of whose birth falls, it is thought, about the years 1529 and 1530, is an artist whose work, in some respects, lies outside the main artistic currents of his age. His birthplace was a small country village near Bergamo and he studied art at Brescia, also in the provinces.

His life seems to have been quite uneventful, that of a conscientious artisan, devoted to his craft. Over a long period, until about 1553, he worked in the studio of the painter Moretto, at Brescia. Since his services were called for by several of the country towns of the province, we may assume that he occasionally travelled. Most of the references to him in chronicles of the period relate to altarpieces he was asked to paint. He died in 1578.

Throughout his career Moroni used, in his religious pictures, themes derived from his teacher's work, and had he confined himself to executing orders of this nature, he would probably have fallen into oblivion, as a mere practitioner of hackneyed methods. It is to his portraits that Moroni owes his fame. In this branch of art he proved himself a master, and won the high esteem of his contemporaries, an esteem we readily endorse today.

To get the best out of himself, Moroni needed the living model. As Mr. Berenson has pointed out there never was in Italy a painter so lacking in the inventive faculty, not to say paralyzed, if he had not a model in front of him. That is so, but we must also recognize that he was far from being deficient in creative power. He makes reality his starting-off point because he aims at re-creating a simple, direct, deliberately restrained and austere pictorial language. Hence his gift of bringing out the individual characteristics of his sitters. He wishes to exhibit them in distinctive attitudes that come quite naturally to them. Probably he was no hand at inventing 'motifs'; his religious compositions—little more than a rehash of his elder, Moretto's themes—suggest this. Yet even here we see touches of originality in some of the portraits he inserts in them, when an opportunity arises.

We must not forget the provincial atmosphere in which he lived, remote from any great art center. His teacher was still expounding and illustrating the 'luminist' and 'mannerist' procedures. And the lesser artists of Venice and her provinces tended to repeat *ad nauseam* the themes of the great masters. Light and color were used solely to produce 'effects,' the limits of space and movement were being recklessly extended, to the point of becoming non-existent. With the result that, in incompetent hands, the composition had developed into mere form devoid of any real content. Thus the discipline Moroni imposed on himself in his portraits was at once a healthy sign and a salutary example.

The function of the light bathing his color harmonies is no longer that of stepping-up their intensity; his light is simplified, subdued, discreet. Nuances and transitions of tones are relatively infrequent, and attuned to the prevailing grey tonality. His sitters belong to all walks of life—a tailor, a soldier, a leading lady of the local bourgeoisie—and he depicts them under their everyday aspects, at work or going about their ordinary avocations. Much praise has been given to the marvelously 'photographic' quality we find in Moroni's portraits; but if there had been no more to his art than this, we should not think so highly of it as we do. Himself a simple, forthright man, the painter succeeded in imparting to the faces of his sitters a pleasant dignity and candor. Perhaps because of his artisan-like way of seeing, Moroni approaches his subjects with a freedom devoid of any social prejudice. "A man's a man for a' that." Anyhow, his sitters, sensible provincials, would not have wanted him to paint them 'in the grand style.' Just as red is the dominant color in Titian's art, so a range of greys, the reflex of his natural modesty, characterizes Moroni's. Thus as between Titian and Moroni, it is the difference between an epic poem on the heroic scale and a humble but delightful 'song of innocence.' It is an interesting fact that Titian advised people at Bergamo to have their portraits painted by Moroni, rather than resort to Venetian artists, and no less interesting that his art inspired some charming sonnets in the local dialect, loud in praises of the painter's skill.

GIAMBATTISTA MORONI (1529/1530-1578). THE TAILOR. (38×29″) NATIONAL GALLERY, LONDON.
REPRODUCED BY COURTESY OF THE TRUSTEES

141

TINTORETTO (1518-1594). CHRIST BEFORE PILATE (DETAIL). SCUOLA DI S. ROCCO, VENICE.

3

LIGHT AND MOVEMENT

TINTORETTO

TINTORETTO (1518-1594). LANDSCAPE, ADAM AND EVE (DETAIL), 1550-1553. ACCADEMIA, VENICE.

TINTORETTO (1518-1594). SUSANNA AND THE ELDERS 1560-1564. (56×75½″) KUNSTHISTORISCHES MUSEUM, VIENNA.

TINTORETTO

"He had a passionate desire for fame and his one thought was to achieve immortality through his work," thus Carlo Ridolfi, writing in the seventeenth century, spoke of Tintoretto. But he sought fame by very different methods from those of Titian, who haunted the great courts of Europe and throughout his life was eager for appreciation in high places. Tintoretto (born in 1518, his real name being Jacopo Robusti), while equally conscious of his genius, devoted himself exclusively to his art.

A man of little culture and lacking social polish, he was frankly 'out to impress'; he wanted his painting to provoke amazement and enthusiasm, but he would not stoop to intrigue, or courting the favor of the great. All he asked was that his work should be exhibited and duly paid for. Though he got orders from Philip II, the King of England and the Gonzagas, he maintained an attitude of sturdy independence, very different from that of Michelangelo, for instance, who still believed that deference was due to patrons. Born in Venice, it was above all in this city that he wished to shine. He was not above filching other men's commissions, on occasion, and though always solicitous for his prestige, never declined orders, even for minor works.

Such being his temperament, it is not surprising that he had few close friends or whole-hearted admirers, and was more criticized than liked. He was blamed for his avarice, and his habit of keeping others at arm's length when he worked was interpreted as disdain

145

TINTORETTO (1518-1594). PORTRAIT OF ALVISE CORNARO. (44×33½″) PITTI PALACE, FLORENCE.

or eccentricity. His private life was uneventful. Married in 1550, he had six children; one of them, his son Domenico, helped him in his work towards the end of his life, and Marietta, a daughter whom he greatly cherished, also had a gift for painting.

It seems that in or about 1539 Tintoretto was apprenticed to Titian. "Tintoretto is said to have stayed only ten days in Titian's house," we are told. Even if his stay there was not so brief as that, it cannot have been a long one, since in this same year Tintoretto was designated 'master painter.' According to one account Titian dismissed him because he was jealous of his pupil's ability, but, given Tintoretto's character, it is more likely that he displayed, even at this early age, his aversion for any sort of control. Nevertheless, Titian's art left an imprint on his pupil. To speak of Titian's 'influence' would be putting it too strongly; what we find in Tintoretto, even in this early stage, is an emphasis laid on colors, in the manner of Titian, but combined with the vigorous delineation of forms characteristic of Michelangelo. We are told that Tintoretto nailed up on his workshop door the sign: "Michelangelo's drawing, Titian's color." Whether this story be true or not, it is significant.

Michelangelo had called into being a whole group of painters aiming exclusively at the exaltation of plastic form. Many such came to Venice, from Florence and elsewhere, and Vasari was one of them. Thus at this time there was a great vogue for what came later to be called 'Michelangelesque Mannerism'. Even Titian was affected by it. Writers of the period tell of the polemics between the two schools of æsthetic thought: one of which laid stress on 'tone' or color values, the other on plastic form. Deliberately, it seems, Tintoretto set out to reconcile these two tendencies. When he exhibited his *Miracle of St Mark* in 1548, it was promptly hailed as a masterpiece; in it the painter had sought, by contrasts of light and shade, to harmonize vigorous draftsmanship and color, and he had succeeded in making a picture which, though stressing the movement of bodies, recalled Titian more than Michelangelo. This was, in fact, his aim: to emphasize the volume of bodies by means of light, but without sacrificing color.

On seeing this work Aretino wrote to the painter, expressing his admiration of the precise rendering of bodies in movement, "less like painting than like life itself." But he demurred at the over-hastiness of the brushwork. Impervious as he was to Titian's 'Impressionism,' he did not realize that Tintoretto's 'impetuous haste' was opening up a new technical approach to art.

A constructive use of light, for the building-up of bodies, is already evident in the *Adam and Eve* (Accademia, Venice), a picture Tintoretto painted, along with two others, between 1550 and 1553, for the Confraternity of the Trinity; here an interplay of light and shade sets the rhythm which gives life to the bodies. And in the successive planes of the landscape, modulations caused by the incidence of light on colors add a curious vibrancy to the atmosphere. Whereas Titian's *Adam and Eve* (in the Prado) shows how far Titian went in blurring form by touches of strong color, Tintoretto uses light to build up volumes. Thus he does not need descriptive line; with him, stresses of light and shade suffice to define the forms of bodies. And while in Titian's rendering of the scene the color is everything and his paradise an enchanted garden, spellbound and serene, Tintoretto both accentuates volumes and imbues all with movement; Adam and Eve, faintly indicated forms, are being driven out by the Angel, a symbolical patch of light, and all nature shares in the action of the drama.

Here the rapidity of the touch, supplying the dynamic element, enables the artist to bring out the tragic violence of the scene, and contrasts with the treatment of the volumes which unfold themselves in an atmosphere of serenity.

Of the many pictures Tintoretto painted during this period none is more renowned than this *Susanna and the Elders* (Vienna), dated 1560-1564 circa, and surely that luminous harmony between the nude figure and its setting could hardly be excelled. Though it takes up over a third of the canvas, the woman's body seems light as a snowflake; and every detail, while stated with precision and attuned to the *ensemble*, is imbued with a soft and starry radiance by the light mirrored in the water and the looking-glass and bringing out such objects as tresses of hair, the little pool with the waterlilies, and the head of the Elder—which, as a contemporary noticed, is rendered "with exceeding wit." Thus what Tintoretto styled his "devotion to reality" is here transmuted into a rhapsody of light.

In 1562 he resumed relations with the Confraternity of St Mark, which had employed him previously (1548), and painted three large pictures of the miracles of St Mark for the Great Hall of this Scuola. These were, doubtless, completed by 1566, when Vasari saw them. Tintoretto was a rapid worker; indeed this rapidity was necessitated by his methods, since, for building up the very fabric of the picture with contrasts of light and dark, he had to produce an impression of rapid movement, sudden clashes. The movement imparted to the figures gives them an elongated aspect, vibrant with an inner life; sometimes these human forms are merely hinted at in a brief flash of light; elsewhere we have robust, fully plastic

TINTORETTO (1518-1594). THE FINDING OF THE BODY OF ST MARK. (159×159″) BRERA, MILAN.

TINTORETTO (1518-1594). CHRIST AT THE SEA OF GALILEE. (46×66½″) KRESS COLLECTION, NATIONAL GALLERY OF ART, WASHINGTON.

bodies. In *The Finding of the Body of St Mark* (Brera) color tends to play a minor part; the vibration of the air is emphasized by an architectural vista, a long recession of silvery arches, and this, so to speak, artificial light, which stresses the figures without enveloping them, together with the general lay-out of the picture gives it the aspect of a majestic 'set' for some romantic drama.

In 1563 the Scuola di San Rocco decided to have the ceiling of their refectory decorated, and several painters (amongst them Veronese) were invited to submit designs. The story of what happened is well known. While the other painters sent in mere sketches, Tintoretto painted the full-size picture, put it up in the place destined to receive it and, out of respect for the saint, made a gift of it to the Confraternity. Naturally enough, the other painters were indignant—but Tintoretto had his way. And for over twenty years he continued working for this Confraternity.

In the great cycle of pictures at the Scuola di San Rocco there are three masterpieces on which the painter worked assiduously: *The Crucifixion, Christ before Pilate,* and *The Way to Golgotha. Christ before Pilate* is famed for its dramatic power; bathed in lambent light, the pale form of Christ stands prominently out, while, a maze of moving shadows, the crowd seethes round it, and massive architecture looms up mysteriously, almost menacingly, through the gloom. All that lies in shadow is treated sketch-wise, sometimes briefly impinging on the field of light, then sinking back into semi-darkness. Forms have become mere symbols, accents, and the color assumes a rich variety of tones: red loaded with shadows, the bluish white of Christ's mantle, masses of black dappled with sudden glints of silver where the light strikes them and giving shadow, the unifying principle, its full value.

TINTORETTO (1518-1594). CHRIST BEFORE PILATE. (216½×159″) SCUOLA DI S. ROCCO, VENICE.

TINTORETTO (1518-1594). THE WAY TO GOLGOTHA. (216½×159″) SCUOLA DI S. ROCCO, VENICE.

TINTORETTO (1518-1594). THE FLIGHT INTO EGYPT. LEFT PART. SCUOLA DI S. ROCCO, VENICE.

TINTORETTO (1518-1594). THE FLIGHT INTO EGYPT. RIGHT PART. SCUOLA DI S. ROCCO, VENICE.

Tintoretto's 'luminist' approach to visual experience enabled him both to body forth reality, the full values of descriptive details, and to develop an infinitely varied range of inventions in the field of painting; thus what strikes the spectator most is the sense of power and the creative zest in all his pictures. In the *Crucifixion*, a vast canvas covering an entire wall, a gyratory movement centers the scene round the form of Christ hanging on the Cross, while those below go about their ordinary occupations. Indeed as Mr. Berenson remarks, "most of the people in the huge canvas are represented, as no doubt they were in life, without much personal feeling about Christ." But, as against this callousness of the human element, the light that bathes this picture is charged with tragic intimations.

Looking at not a few of Tintoretto's works, we might be led to read into them the expression of some strong religious emotion actually experienced by the artist. But there was nothing of the mystic in Tintoretto's personality; he was too much in love with life, perhaps, or too proud. Thus Ruskin said of him that he sometimes forgot himself to the point of seeming pious, but in fact he practiced the same method as Titian: a complete subordination of the religious subject to decoration and the portrait. A generation later El Greco, starting from the premises supplied by Tintoretto, was to transpose them on to another level and, with a sensibility quite alien to the Italian creative artists of this period, to succeed in giving mysticism one of the loftiest expressions it has ever known.

During his next period Tintoretto worked in the Great Hall, whose decoration he undertook in 1576. Next year, in the months of January, March and September, he submitted further plans to the Confraternity, with the result that the ceiling and walls ended by being entirely clothed with painting. These additional works, illustrating scenes from the Old and New Testaments, were brought to a conclusion in 1580-81.

TINTORETTO (1518-1594). THE FALL OF MANNA (DETAIL). CHURCH OF S. GIORGIO MAGGIORE, VENICE.

TINTORETTO (1518-1594). THE ASCENSION (DETAIL). SCUOLA DI S. ROCCO, VENICE.

Tintoretto continued working here till about 1580, and meanwhile his genius progressed from strength to strength. Though here and there a detail is treated in a realistic manner, he now transmutes reality into a grandiose vision, a supernal world of light.

155

Painter of light, Tintoretto was ever seeking after movement; he wanted the action to have no end. One might almost say he wished to perpetuate it beyond the space of the canvas; indeed the whole atmosphere seems charged with life, illimited, untrammelled. The image-movement is presented in diverse manners, so as to interpret all aspects of reality. In *The Adoration of the Shepherds*, for example, the scene is cut transversally into two superimposed planes by a beam of the stable, enabling us to see two sequences of events following and complementing each other. Similarly in *The Ascension* we see consecutive events

TINTORETTO (1518-1594). THE ANNUNCIATION (DETAIL). SCUOLA DI S. ROCCO, VENICE.

TINTORETTO (1518-1594). ST ROCCO HEALING THE SICK (DETAIL). CHURCH OF S. ROCCO, VENICE.

occurring in the same space, the time dimension being expressed by an arrangement of planes. Bodies swirl in the thickly crowded sky and their density is measured by their luminosity, while the two apostles in the landscape which gives its balance to the scene produce an impression of vibrations faintly tinted pink and yellow. The romantic side of Tintoretto's art has often been remarked on. His compositions, whose boldness must have startled his contemporaries, pointed the way to a new pictorial world and heralded Baroque.

However, this tendency toward what might be called spectacular representation, built of theatrical effects, emphatic contrasts that plunge the figures into a world of violent movement, often rendered with downward foreshortenings and glimpsed in flashes of light or pools of shadow, gives place to a calmer mood, infused with gentle emotion, in the pictures, made probably between 1583 and 1587, for the ground floor of the Scuola. In all alike, the *Flight into Egypt*, the *Magdalen in the Desert* and most notably in *Mary the Egyptian*, landscape plays a leading part. And what strikes us in these works is not so much the rendering of nature—water, trees and sky—as the artist's new sense of the all-pervading atmosphere. Thus the composition of *The Flight into Egypt* is so arranged as to enable the light freely to bathe in its silvery sheen the rich diversity of the landscape. And the figures of the Virgin and St Joseph seem to be moving out of the canvas, faintly touched with light, so as to leave the sunset free to enfold in a luminous embrace the sky and the distant cottage.

The San Rocco decorations form a truly impressive group, and have often been compared to Michelangelo's series of paintings in the Sistine and Masaccio's in the Brancacci Chapel. From the moment it was completed this majestic work elicited enthusiastic praise from painters and connoisseurs alike. We need only recall Velazquez' expression of his admiration for it, as recorded by Boschini in his *Carta del Navegar pittoresco*.

Though the colors have dulled with the years, San Rocco still eloquently testifies to the greatness of this rare artist who, more perhaps here than in any of his other works, makes us feel the visionary sweep of his creative genius.

TINTORETTO (1518-1594). VULCAN'S FORGE (DETAIL). DUCAL PALACE, VENICE.

But the painter did not confine himself to work on the Scuola di San Rocco; he also had many commissions from the authorities at Venice. *The Last Judgement* and *The Battle of Lepanto*, made for the Doge's Palace, were destroyed in the 1577 fire. Also during this period the painter completed four pictures for the 'Square Room,' of the Palace; these were to symbolize and extol the glory of Venice. Actually he used the theme as an opportunity for a symptuous display of women's forms; ethereal yet sensuously real, they weave in air a pattern of fluent arabesques. Very different is *Vulcan's Forge*, which symbolized the union of the Venetian senators in the administration of the state; here the dynamic lighting stresses the robustness of the male bodies, whose muscles stretch and twist in an all-embracing rhythm. As against Michelangelo's, Tintoretto's art is a glorification of light as that which imparts to bodies their intensest life. And Tintoretto's great discovery was a special kind of light which, in its interplay with shadow, sometimes disintegrates from and sometimes, in stressing the full value of bodies, builds it up. Movements, whether fast or slow, are continuous and their undulations are adjusted to the purport of the composition, illustrative or dramatic. True, Tintoretto is a colorist; but his color, always dissolving into shadow, is thus deprived of vividness; indeed it has no function independently of light. Sometimes it is faintly silvered, elsewhere richly steeped in shadow, darkly glowing.

About 1586-1590 Tintoretto painted an enormous panel, *Paradise*, for the Doge's Palace. While the picture itself, if only because of its unwieldy size, fails to achieve a perfect harmony of forms and colors in the chiaroscuro, the sketch in the Louvre shows to advantage the buoyant freedom of those rotatory movements which are drawing up small color patches, higher and ever higher, into the sky. In 1594, the year of his death, Tintoretto painted a *Deposition* for the mortuary chapel of S. Giorgio Maggiore, and in it he proved that "old age notwithstanding," as Ridolfi writes, "this hand which had wrought so many miracles had not lost its cunning." He left some uncompleted works; as we learn from his Will, he was much perturbed at the thought of what might be done to them after his death.

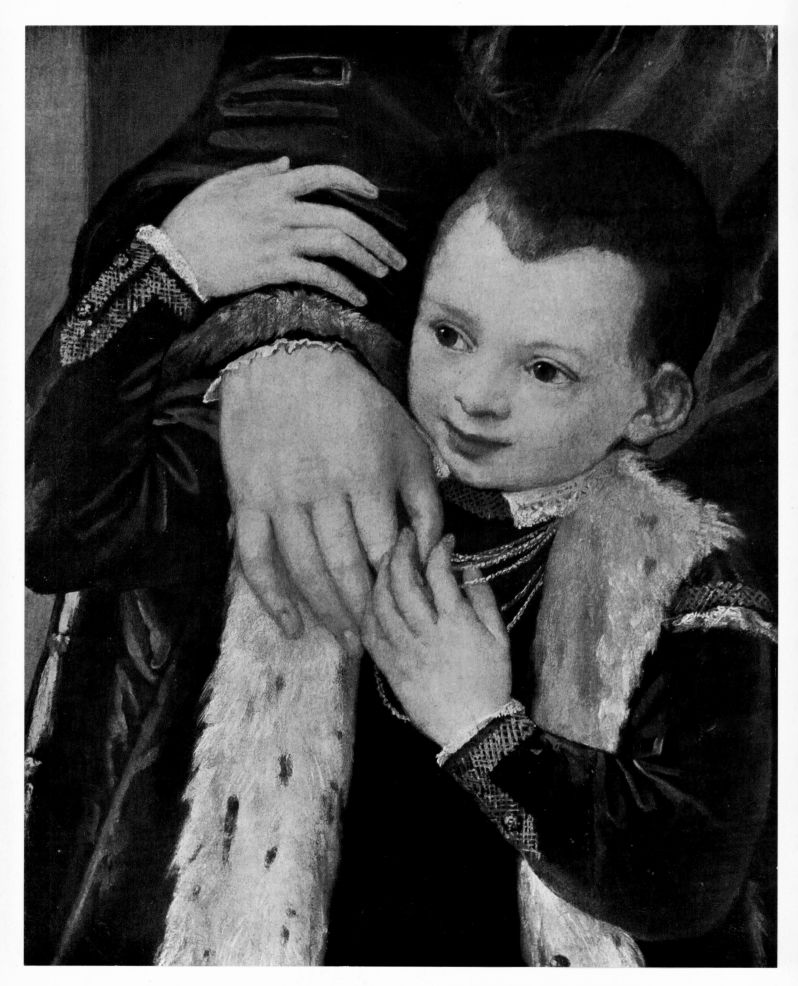

PAOLO VERONESE (1528-1588). PORTRAIT OF COUNT DA PORTO AND HIS SON (DETAIL).
COLLECTION OF COUNT CONTINI BONACOSSI, FLORENCE.

THE TRIUMPH OF COLOR

VERONESE

PAOLO VERONESE (1528-1588). HEAD, ST MENNAS (DETAIL). GALLERIA D'ESTE, MODENA.

VERONESE

"We might do worse than count up all the touches of his brush as if they were so many pearls, sapphires, emeralds, all the most precious jewels of the East." Thus Boschini wrote, speaking of Veronese, and indeed this is much what we feel when gazing at this great artist's pictures, with their magical colors, glittering lights, sumptuous, decorative figures. Born in 1528, Veronese was the most typically Venetian of artists; his painting is a mirror held to the brilliant, sparkling life, the opulence and gaiety of Venice in her heyday.

Paolo Caliari's birthplace was Verona; hence the name of 'Veronese' by which he is generally known. Verona was under the sway of Venice and her fame as an art center in the great days of Altichiero, then of Pisanello, was already of the past. At the end of the fifteenth and the beginning of the sixteenth century, painting at Verona was a curious mixture of conflicting influences, with Mantegna's predominating. Amongst the painters of the period we may mention Giovanni Caroto (1480-1555) who, while much influenced by Bellini and Mantegna, discovered for himself a grace of form resembling Raphael's. And indeed during this first half of the sixteenth century, the art of the Veronese painters often displays what are—allowance made for the provincial setting—personal and original traits. They invented a sort of mannerism, which (if we discount the influences of Titian and Giorgione) links up with some of the schematic methods of Giulio Romano, then working at Mantua. Such, in brief, was the background of Paolo Caliari's early years.

An early work (1552), an altarpiece for the Mantua Cathedral (commissioned by Cardinal Gonzaga), shows how quick he was to assimilate the new tendencies in art. Though he came of humble stock—his father was a stonebreaker—he had an innate love of elegance, and there was so much of the *grand seigneur* in his approach to art that when in 1555 he painted the sacristy ceiling at the Church of S. Sebastiano, even the Venetians were vastly impressed. A painter born, he seemed in full possession of his artistic personality from the start, and implicit in it was the very spirit of Venice. For him, Venice was the city of great palaces then being built along the Grand Canal; the home of a cultured aristocracy who wanted their interiors richly, even lavishly, adorned—in short a city whose gay elegance was a reflection, as it were, of the brilliant light of the lagoon. This was not Titian's Venice, eager to retain its power, its wealth and its pre-eminence in art, nor Tintoretto's city of unrest, swept by storms and dazzling sunbursts. Veronese had no wish to impart any moral or social significance to his pictures. He set down, without a second thought, his visual experience, and, being gifted with superb creative imagination, has given the world a series of works which, behind their decorative aspect, have a very real grandeur. With seeming-casual touches and in frank, brilliant colors he painted big canvases crowded with people, animals and objects, or made decorations on the walls of country mansions, in which we see elegant figures, rendered with illusionist realism, leaning over balconies, stepping forth from doorways, exactly as in life. Even in his smaller pictures he conveys an impression of boundless space, and every color tells out strongly, bathed in shimmering light.

We have little, outside his work, to throw light on the temperament of this painter, with the exception of a remarkable incident that took place in 1573. In that year he was summoned before the tribunal of the Inquisition, in connection with a painting, the *Feast in the House of Levi* (the Last Supper), made for the refectory of the Confraternity of SS. Giovanni and Paolo. The charge was that of treating sacred subjects in an irreligious, worldly manner. Veronese faced the issue squarely, not only vindicating the creative freedom of the artist but asserting his belief that painting should be governed by its own laws only. Thus when he was asked why he had painted soldiers clad in the German style and carrying such 'modern' weapons as halberds, he replied: "We painters take the same liberties as poets and madmen. So I painted these halberdiers, one eating, the other drinking, because I thought their presence was called for, and also because it seemed only right that an influential, well-to-do householder should have many servitors." Again, when the judges asked him

PAOLO VERONESE (1528-1588). THE MARRIAGE AT CANA (DETAIL), 1562-1563. LOUVRE, PARIS.

who, in his opinion, were likely to have been present at the Feast, his answer was: "I believe that Christ and the apostles were there; but whenever an empty space in the picture needs filling up, I put in figures as the fancy takes me." And, to prove that painters always do as they like, Veronese cited the case of Michelangelo who painted nudes on the walls of the Sistine. But these arguments failed to convince the Inquisitors, who ordered the artist to rectify the picture at his own expense. Veronese was both versatile and a quick worker; he not only kept up a steady output of easel-pictures, but turned his hand to large-scale decorations, for he liked having big surfaces to work on. He resumed work at the Church of S. Sebastiano (where he had already painted, in 1555, the sacristy ceiling) and continued working there until 1570 and later. His great talent had been recognized by the Venetians, and notably by Titian, when in 1556-1557 he painted three *tondi* for the library of S. Marco, built by Sansovino. He worked for several churches and painted many huge pictures

PAOLO VERONESE (1528-1588). ST JOHN THE BAPTIST. (81½×55″) GALLERIA BORGHESE, ROME.

PAOLO VERONESE (1528-1588). VENUS AND MARS. (18½×19″) GALLERIA SABAUDA, TURIN.

of feasts, most famous of which are the *Marriage at Cana* and the *Feast in the House of Levi*. At a date which cannot be precisely fixed he did frescos in the villa Barbaro-Giacomelli at Maser (near Treviso): a composition of dazzling brilliance with its luminous blue skies, and infinite expanses in which the figures, portrayed under everyday aspects yet with an elegance transcending that of ordinary mortals, illustrate themes of mythology or allegory. In these figures and in the landscapes unfurled along the walls, we see a prodigious imagination at work, and an almost magical power of making colors scintillate like gems, bathed in a light intenser than the light of day.

Between 1575 and 1577 he painted the ceiling of the Collegio in the Doge's Palace; ensconced in richly gilded recesses of the coffered ceiling, the stately figures of the Virtues shine forth, clad in a radiance of celestial light.

When Veronese died in 1588, he had given the world an immense quantity of works of the highest order. The strange thing is that, except perhaps in his last phase, his style shows no development. On the other hand, his imaginative power never failed him, all his life long he invented new 'motives'; with the result that his vast output strikes us as infinitely varied, full of new discoveries as to details and new arrangements as to the *ensemble*. But the artistic personality of the man who worked these wonders never varied. Just as he never knew the qualms so many artists feel regarding their vocation, so he never felt an impulse to break through his limitations and go in quest of new horizons. From his very first paintings he felt quite sure of himself, equipped with all his means of expression, and though gaining experience on the way, he always followed the same path. What delights us in his art is its frank expression of the joy of living and the artist's response to all that made the beauty and the splendor of the world around him. Thus his big religious compositions are in the nature of gorgeous pageants; there is nothing biblical about them, they reflect the Venetian scene at its most luxurious. It was this 'modernity' in his treatment of sacred subjects that so much shocked the Inquisition; his representation of such a subject as the *Last Supper* brings to mind a festival taking place in some Venetian township, in which the artist has brought together a crowd of figures, a plethora of ornaments and details; where colors are given their utmost luminosity by contrasts of tones, and even shadows are not black but colored—with the result that light seems welling up from everything, opening up ever vaster depths of space. This is why he so often uses architectural motives to implement those long recessions which enable him to make his figures stand out, clean-cut silhouettes, against an illimitable sky. Moreover, Veronese lingers on every detail, exalts it, imparts to it a value of its own; with the result that these huge decorative compositions give the spectator an enhanced delight when he lets his eyes rest on each group, attitude and object, separately. Each of the persons in them has his own role, each is individualized. Thus in the *St Mennas* (Modena), the saint is given a concave, niche-like background, from which he seems to be stepping forth, and the maximum of light is concentrated on each part of the picture. Hence, too, his exceptional power of rendering the texture of materials, the shimmering luster of richly embroidered garments. But Veronese does not confine himself to the purely decorative aspects of the scenes he paints. In his best works he imbues them with an incomparable elegance and a truly poetic glamor; we feel we are witnessing a vision of life at once serene and dazzling in its beauty. Thus in the *Deposition* the glorification of vivid color against the infinite recession of the sky does not strike a tragic note; for, though so poignantly felt by the artist, the divine tragedy is sublimated, lifted to a plane where joy and sorrow have no place, withdrawn into a high, transcendent world of light.

A mood of happiness unruffled by misgivings is what we find in Veronese's art. Its wealth of perfectly harmonious colors—colors that 'sing' with never a jarring note—and its well-tempered, spacious rhythms led some to see in it a classical stability, while others claimed that Veronese opened windows on fields of art as yet uncharted. Actually, however, the century and its creative urge (so far as its great painters are concerned) ended with Veronese. The interests of the next century, a phase of almost frenzied sensibility, lay elsewhere, though some of its artists took over from Veronese such elements as served the prevailing trend towards a plethora of decoration.

We are almost tempted to see in the sixteenth century a singular venture: an attempt by man to assert his power in art at the very time when, on the factual level, it was experiencing so many setbacks.

Leonardo's restless temperament had prompted him to research-work in every field; Raphael's life was dedicated to an ideal of beauty. And though Michelangelo defiantly asserted the power of man, the Venetians, from Giorgione to Tintoretto, employed all the nuances of tones, the vibrations of color and of light in hymning their feeling for reality, while Tintoretto imparted to his vision of the world a glamor of a somewhat theatrical nature. Then, with the coming of Veronese, painting took on a new lease of life; his talent was immense, his proficiency seemed limitless. All the earlier discoveries were recapitulated in his art; combining high technical accomplishment with an extreme sensitivity to color, he achieved a marvelous efficiency of portrayal, immobilized, one might almost say, in the contemplation of its own beauty. His unfaltering faith in his genius and the freedom with which he envisaged his mission enabled Veronese to renew art. Thus he stood for a summing-up and culmination of all the tendencies of a century, and it was difficult to go farther on the path that he had charted. When we mark the subtle relations he created between tones and his telling contrasts we have a feeling that a host of hitherto undreamt-of nuances arise spontaneously from his canvases. Indeed a color was named after Veronese.

Great was the debt that eighteenth-century art owed to this painter who brought the Venetian Cinquecento to a triumphal close with his visions of the enchanted radiance of the lagoons.

PAOLO VERONESE (1528-1588). THE CRUCIFIXION. (40×40″) LOUVRE, PARIS.

THIS,

THE FIFTH VOLUME OF THE COLLECTION

" PAINTING ∘ COLOR ∘ HISTORY "

WAS PRODUCED
BY THE TECHNICAL STAFF OF EDITIONS D'ART ALBERT SKIRA.
FINISHED THE FIRST DAY OF JULY,
NINETEEN HUNDRED AND SIXTY-ONE.

COLORPLATES BY

SKIRA

COLOR STUDIOS AT IMPRIMERIES RÉUNIES, LAUSANNE.
TEXT PRINTED BY IMPRIMERIE CENTRALE, LAUSANNE.

PRINTED IN SWITZERLAND